The Book of Being...

Your Playbook on How to Be Happy & Win at the Game of Life!

THE BOOK OF BEING...

ISBN-9781073388035

Published by Aware Consulting Services

THE BOOK OF BEING...

TABLE OF CONTENTS

"The moment when you really experience that you have
created yourself being whatever way you are, at that
same moment you will never have to be that way again."

Werner Erhard

DEDICATION

Before we get into the heart of this undertaking: *The Book of Being*, indulge me for a minute and let's take a little stroll down memory lane...

When I began this project several years ago, I was returned to a day in 1982 - *I think it was in April* - that I first heard the word "transformation."

I sat in a room with 200 or more people, listening to someone (arrogant, forceful and charismatic) at the front of the room, informing me that IF I intended to complete this event, I was going to spend the next two weekends of my life, and several additional evenings, being told how often and when I could eat, go to the bathroom and, essentially, find out what a waste my life had been up to that point. In fact, I soon found out, that I was also to be told in no uncertain terms, what an asshole I was - AND, in addition, that I didn't even know that ***particular* aperture** from a hole in the ground.

Little did I know, in that moment, that the direction of my life would change forever and that I would never be the same.

Dedication (Cont'd)

The work or "training" as it was known in its earliest permutation, was known as **est,** created by a man called **Werner Erhard** (formerly Jack Rosenberg).

Back then, in the beginning, we entrusted them - Werner, the Forum Leaders and staff - with our egos, our hearts, our minds and our highest Selves, hoping to experience that illusive, enticing, empowering "transformation" that would, hopefully and ultimately, change our lives forever.

The work Werner began in the 70's has since undergone many changes from those early days; both in name and some of the practices it employed while delivering its transformative education.

For one thing, you will never - in these days - hear that same scatological language (known as "cursing," to those of my generation). Many of those changes were instituted by him, while other changes were made by those to whom he later handed off his organization and its programs; the heart of which is now known as The Landmark Forum, now delivered by Landmark Worldwide and delivered by 52 extraordinary individuals around the world, known as Forum Leaders.

The Forum - and the many other programs that followed - which they now call "The Curriculum for Living," as well as the parent Organization have grown and changed over the years, much as have

Dedication (Cont'd)

the "senior graduates" - participants, like me and thousands of others. However, with all its many changes - and through its maturation process - this work has made a world of difference to millions of people and countless organizations on the planet.

It is to this man, this amazing human being, who has made such a difference in my life and in the millions of lives who came before and after me, that I dedicate this program.

Everything you will read or experience or see here, is sourced by what I was given in those first, early days of the est training and for which I remain forever grateful.

Thank you, Werner, for being willing to blaze the trail for all those who came after you with their programs, their ideas, their commitment to transformation.

While others may not acknowledge it, all of us who sat in those rooms with hundreds of strangers those many years ago, recognizing our connected hearts, experiencing our deepest commitments and acknowledging our shared humanity, it is clear that you laid the track; making it possible for all of us continue our journey into enlightenment and transformation.

And now... on with the show!

Invent a Whole New Paradigm

Be Present

Take 100% Responsibility

Affirm Actions Assignments Practice

Transformation

PREAMBLE TO BOOK OF BEING

Your Playbook on How to Be Happy & Win the Game of Life!

Our Commitment: To provide you with access to transformation, complete self-expression and a global community committed to peace and well-being for everyone.

However, before you continue, I am going to ask one more thing of you.

Preamble (cont'd)

STOP and take a deep breath!

This program comes with a warning.

This is NOT an "Easy, light-hearted, how-to," book or program that you can breeze through and be amused by. If that is why you picked it up, return it immediately - access it no further; **it is definitely not what you are looking for and it will be a waste of your time and money!**

If you are prepared for a journey into the unknown... into creating - with us - a new possibility for your life and for the lives of everyone who knows you, keep going.

THAT is the core of what you are about to undertake as you proceed through The Book of Being.

Got it?

If you still want to continue; if you are still intrigued and up for the challenge? Keep Going... and *WELCOME!*

PRE-INTRODUCTION

As you begin this program, it is important that you listen to - or read - the following introduction.

Why?

It may help if we first tell you what the Introduction is NOT.

It is not a preamble to the "good stuff" beyond...

It is not a disposable, throwaway conversation that can be skipped to get to the meat of the conversations that follow. In short, it is NOT an *'amuse bouche'* for the program ahead. Your first assignment (*There will be assignments*) is to check out what that means in the dictionary if you don't already know.

Here is what the Introduction IS.

The Introduction, is the set-up for learning. **It is the foundation for building transformation and the heartbeat of all else to follow.** (Another warning...**Stop now** if you are not ready to take on the transformation of life as you know it and, ultimately, transformation of the planet Earth.

If you are ready, so are we... Begin by reading the Introduction.

"One's destination is never a place, but a new way of seeing things."

Henry Miller

INTRODUCTION

[Careful...I can hear you saying "Finally!"]

As author, creator and self-appointed guide on your journey, I can only assume you, adventuresome reader, have purchased this program in hopes of learning about "Being." Perhaps you are intrigued because you have heard about transformation, or ontology, or one of the mind-tickling words or phrases used in our marketing or visual descriptions of this program.

I AM, however, confident (and arrogant?) enough in what I have to offer, to assume you really have no idea what you are about to undertake by engaging with this information. By the way, we purposefully say "engaging with this information" rather than "reading" it or "listening" to it because those activities (listening and reading) are such a small part of the experience I intend for you to have as a result of your having made this purchase.

I have plans for you... and for the planet. So, get comfortable (for a few minutes only) and let's begin your journey. You have my word that your comfort is likely to last only a short while, so enjoy it while you can. Many of the things we will be exploring together are guaranteed, by their nature, to make you *UN*comfortable; so, for the time being, relax and engage in a few conversations that will begin your journey into what we mean when we say "Being."

Introduction (Cont'd)

The journey begins with a few words about how this program will be laid out. There will be multiple "working definitions" throughout. **Working definitions** are distinct from definitions you may find in Webster's dictionary or WikiDicky or whatever online resource you may use to define words for yourself or others.

Working definitions are "agreed upon (by specifically involved individuals) meanings of a word or phrase." While these words or phrases may be commonly used in the English language, you will find the definitions I give them to be quite distinct and, for our purpose and intentions, powerfully useful in the work we will be doing together.

Nearly every chapter will have in it "*working definitions*" of some sort so we want to be clear what we mean by that.

Let's begin with our first "working definition" for **Ontology** because that is the foundation for the transformative work we are about to undertake here.

Introduction (Cont'd)

As it turns out, our first "working definition" parallels pretty closely the publicly accepted definition given by Merriam Webster: Ontology: A particular theory about the nature of being or the kinds of things that have existence. A branch of metaphysics concerned with the nature and relations of being.

Basically then, "Ontology," which is the conversation in which we will be dwelling for much of this program, is the philosophical study of the nature of human *being, becoming, existence*, or *reality*, as well as the basic categories of being and their relations.

To put it simply (which we will not always be able to do in this book so take advantage of when we do) ... is the study of "**what it is to be a human" for Human Beings.**

Got it? Good. We will be exploring that a LOT.

One more thing – while we will be exploring LOTS of different ways of being for Human Beings, nothing we will say is "THE TRUTH." So, if you are looking for "THE TRUTH," you've come to the wrong place.

Introduction (Cont'd)

We will be asking you to "try on" many different ideas, concepts, ways of looking at life, at living, at thinking; and we won't ask you to "believe" any of it. ONLY to consider and to try on (like a jacket) some of these ideas and concepts and see if they will work for you.

My only desire is to empower you to explore the possibilities I present and then decide for yourself if they will make the kind of difference for you – in YOUR life – as they have made in mine.

So, to continue on the subject of "What it is to be a human being." The being of human beings. Seems a bit odd to even consider that, doesn't it? What do we mean by the "being" of human beings?

Mostly, if you think about it, we consider the things that people DO to be the nature of human beings. It is, after all, actually one of the first things we ask someone that we have just met, "and... what do you do" (as in "for a living")?

Isn't that how others define us? **How we frequently define ourselves and one another?** What do you do? In that way, we get a sense of "who" someone is... by what they DO. Consider then, that common question of **"Why we are not called human doings instead of human beings?"** I know, overused and frequently a comment of self-

Introduction (Cont'd)

appointed gurus throughout the ages... a throwaway line used by many of us as well; **but have we really given it the kind of thought it deserves?**

Why *are* we so busy "doing" all the time? What drives that "doingness" - that need to create our identity from what we produce and what we do? Is there an answer to that and is it at all useful? Stay tuned!

By the way, we will be saying that a lot probably - **"Stay tuned."** We ask a lot more questions than we give answers... especially in the beginning, so you may want to develop the patience of Job to get through all the questions we will be posing for you. You may even start to appreciate them halfway through...

Get used to it.

Introduction (Cont'd)

Moving right along - So, now you have been introduced to Ontology and ontological conversations and that questions will become the order of the day as you move forward in this book. You are learning a lot already and we aren't halfway through the Introduction!

Now, primarily as you read the material in this program, you will mostly be reading my words. And, what you should know is that there was actually a "we" when I began this project and that was my partner or colleague and I, who began creating this program together.

Although he, Geoff Owen, was an integral part of this conversation in the beginning, he has moved on to other things; however, I want to make sure his contribution to me and to the beginning of this journey is recognized. Thanks, Geoff - and I hope you are well and creating a most wonderful future for yourself.

So, now, moving on, let's continue with the "ontological" conversation with which we began this Introduction.

And, though you won't be hearing much from Geoff as we continue, he did instruct me to assure you that while I've pretty much nailed the distinction Ontology, for him - for most of his life - "being" was definitely about "doing."

Introduction (Cont'd)

You probably understand how that goes: If I **do** this (go to school, get a great position, meet and marry the right person etc.), I'll **have** what I want (a degree, experience and knowledge, good money and promotions, a perfect partner) and then I'll **be** this... (happy, satisfied, successful, fulfilled) ...sort of the 'roundabout' thing that almost all of us experience. BUT, and here's the crucial thing - Geoff said- and I think you can agree - few of us know that there is any other way! **That's just the "way it is!"**

If you...

1. **Do** the right thing so...
2. You can **HAVE** the things that you want and...
3. You will **BE** who you want to be; happy, fulfilled and satisfied!

Right? I'm not so sure... I'm actually going to ask you to consider... That this formula - the one most of us follow our whole lives - **frequently does NOT work!** I'm going to ask you to consider that there could be another way... Stay tuned for that - it's coming in a future chapter!

Most of us have little awareness that what we are doing isn't working until it is almost too late! We are so focused on the 'doing'

Introduction (Cont'd)

part of life (and many of us very successfully, I might add); the achieving "in order to" get that 'missing something' that everyone else on the planet seems to have mastered but us. And that, really for most of us, can be the truly confronting thing.

All along, we think that what we are doing is what we are "supposed" to do as human beings and, therefore, we accept our experience as the default experience of being human. It is this **default paradigm** that mostly drives our day-to-day behavior - and it's the reason I have chosen to share what I've have learned with you today.

One of the things we will be doing a lot as we proceed on this journey together is to explore words, their meanings and how they impact our way of "being" in the world.

Let's take a look at a word you will hear a lot as you move through this program; and that word is **"distinctions."** *Distinctions* differ from *working definitions,* which we described earlier, in that they do not "describe" or define something; they "distinguish" - or make it "pop" could be another way to describe it. They allow you to become aware of something that, before that moment you discovered it, you had no idea it existed. **Sometimes people refer to these things as "Aha's!" or insights.**

Let me give you an example.

Introduction (Cont'd)

Observe the picture below. What do you see? A Roller Coaster? A child or two? Look again... What else? a carousel? You may have experienced something similar to this before - perhaps in a children's book... Take a closer look. Consider that there may be something here that bears resemblance to a top hat? Ice Cream cone? Perhaps a banana? Check out this list of "hidden Objects" and see what you can find in the picture. Circle or highlight them...Take a few minutes to do this... then continue reading.

[Find a top hat, butterfly, sailboat, teacup, open book, bell, pencil, ice cream cone, banana, penguin, grapes and boot]

Introduction (Cont'd)

Did you find them? Are you now able to "see the picture" differently? So why did we have you do that? What can you possibly learn from a children's drawing of "hidden objects"?

What you have just done is participate in an exercise designed to have you experience (in a simplistic way, of course), something that was previously hidden from your view.

That is, by being willing to look at something in a new way or by opening your view of something, you literally made the *invisible, visible*. That is what **distinctions** provide; a new view of life, of circumstances that you thought were one way and, then, by considering a new way of seeing something, or we would say "distinguishing something" you can actually have a different perspective or view of something you only saw one way before. And, amazingly enough, once you distinguish something for yourself, once you see a new dimension, it is always accessible afterwards.

One powerful example of a distinction many of us experience early on in life was very effectively demonstrated by Werner Erhard in what used to be the est training. As you know from reading the dedication, **Werner was my first teacher in the area of "personal development" and he described it this way:**

Introduction (Cont'd)

How to ride a bike: You must have balance to ride a bike. It's true, you can "tell" someone how to ride a bike. You can describe how to steer, how to peddle, how to avoid falling by steering toward the direction you seem to be falling. You can explain and give them all the necessary instructions on how to balance themselves, and an explanation of what balance is; but, and only, once they get ON the bike, and attempt to ride it, can they actually "experience" balance. **Balance is a distinction.** That is the way of distinctions. You can describe them, talk about them and what they are and what they are not, but until someone experiences them - it is difficult to make them real. **And, as you have heard over the years, once you have "distinguished"** *balance* **by riding a bike, you never forget!** *Thanks, Werner!*

In this program, I will be attempting to describe some powerful distinctions (*like balance*) for you; distinctions that can truly transform your life AND, chances are, that unless and until you actually put these things into practice in your life, you will not truly experience the power of these words.

That is why I am telling you - in this introduction - that until and unless you are really willing to engage with what I tell you – to take action when I coach you to do so, what you experience and learn here will have little or no impact on your life.

Introduction (Cont'd)

It will just be one more "self-help, self-enlightenment, self-indulgent attempt to change or improve" your circumstances. My advice: please do not do that to yourself. Don't waste your time, the time it took to write this book or your money. **Put it back now and buy yourself some light reading, or**... accept my invitation.

Take this opportunity to truly transform your existence. Take your daily, ordinary, trudging through life and stick it where the sun doesn't shine! **Take action** and create a whole new domain of possibility for yourself and what is possible for the people you love in your life.

I am rooting for you!

Ready to take it on? Great! Let's go!

Next up is **Chapter 1 of the 10 Transformational Empowerments...It's all ME, all the way up and all the way down!!**

EMPOWERMENT CHAPTER 1

"It's All ME: All the Way Up and All the Way Down!!

(and that's the good news!)

So, now that we've established that you are ready to begin this journey to transformation, let's take a look at the foundational premise upon which it is all built.

You could think about it this way…

If you've ever participated in building a house, either directly or indirectly, you know the first thing that happens after plans are made is that construction workers lay a foundation. First the ground is leveled, and sand is poured across the level ground. Then, supports are put in place around the sand and cement is poured into that support structure.

Now, provided the cement cures properly and there are no cracks or imperfections, your foundation is established, and construction of your new building can begin. Of course, if there are cracks in the foundation then there will, in time, be cracks in the walls and, eventually, the building will collapse.

Chapter 1 (Cont'd)

That's why the foundation is such a critical piece of a building's integrity. And so it goes with the foundation of this program - and of your life.

With regard to how the material in this program is designed, Chapter 1 will be about setting up the parameters and guidelines for what will be required from you to achieve the success that is possible for you as you actively engage in your assignments. In other words, Chapter 1 sets up the foundation for your transformation.

As you take action, observe and engage with the material, you will begin to see the possibility that you are creating in your life and that you have the potential to be powerful beyond your current understanding.

You will see that by engaging in the questions we ask, by being willing to go past where you have gone before and what you have believed to be true about yourself, and in your willingness to question what is possible for you, you will find an unpredictable extraordinary future.

Chapter 1 (Cont'd)

At the end of every Empowerment Chapter, you will have assignments - called AffirmActions - activities and exercises - which will be required before you can move on to the next Chapter. Now, of course, I won't be there to "make" you do anything. You are on your own insofar as that is concerned. However, IF you want to get out of this program what you want to get, those AffirmActions and assignments ARE required.

By the way, I'll be explaining soon what an AffirmAction is, so stay tuned...

Also, throughout the program, questions will be posed for you to answer and activities to engage in at that moment. **Your job is to answer these questions at the moment you encounter them.**

Do NOT read ahead. **Let me repeat that... Do NOT read ahead.** Answer the questions and complete the activities as you come upon them in the program. Why? Because they are there for a reason and that reason will become abundantly clear as you begin to build some muscles in "being" (Remember... the name of the program is "Book of Being").

Chapter 1 (Cont'd)

SO, that brings us to your FIRST assignment... While this program is designed as a book or workbook in which you can write, I also recommend that you get yourself an additional diary or a notebook of some kind in which you can add additional notes. While for some of you, this book will be sufficient, for others of you, having a notebook or journal in which to write will be highly beneficial.

My suggestion is that it be a beautiful journal or book, bound in some way, with a hardcover; one that you love the feel of and that you will want to write in... A journal with a substantial number of pages, or one to which you can easily add pages. Or, you could get a series of notebooks, one for each Chapter. Whatever you choose, make sure it is sturdy and easy to get to. Also, keep close to you a favorite pen or writing instrument that will last throughout your journey.

Let's talk here for a moment about these end of Empowerment Chapter "Assignments."

The first thing to get is that if you do only part of an assignment, you did not do the assignment. **Doing part of them is not doing the assignment. If you do not do the assignment, you give up the right to expect the results.**

Chapter 1 (Cont'd)

Now, you *may* get the results anyway – you could be lucky. But, if you truly want to experience a transformation in your life, you will have to do 100% of the assignments. That's just the way this works. You don't have to like it, you just have to do them. If you don't do them, you will want to notice where else in your life do you do things 'halfway' and what kind of results you are getting. Are they the kind of results you want to keep getting? Probably not. So, this program is an opportunity to "raise the bar" – Do you know what that means?

It means try on a new way of being that raises what you have at stake in engaging in this program. It means keeping your word – and doing what you said you would do. Each time you do that, you will progress to another level of mastery. Is that pretty clear? Great!

And I want to emphasize that you aren't wrong or bad if you don't do it – you just won't get the results... That is the simplest way I can put it. You can read all the pages, think about all the information and even do some of the required work... and, if you DON'T do the assignments in their entirety, you will not, in all likelihood, get the results that are possible for you; so, I really invite you to take on these assignments and AffirmActions as if your life depended on it – because literally, the expanded quality of your life *will* depend on it.

Chapter 1 (Cont'd)

So now, let's take a moment to explore your expectations. You purchased this program with a certain objective or expectation about what it would provide for you - and its title "Book of Being" certainly led to you to believe that what it would deliver was in the domain of "Being" - correct?

Consider first, the following areas of your life... and where you experience satisfaction and dissatisfaction... Check where you feel completely satisfied and feel free to make a short note or comment where you do not.

Recognition:
☐ **Where do you feel "unappreciated" or not recognized enough in your life?**
For example, name one thing that you would want acknowledgement or recognition for which you have not yet - or ever – received? Something you believe you do well and yet no one else has commented on or noticed it.

_____

_____

_____

_____

_____

_____

Chapter 1 (Cont'd)

_____
_____
_____

Self-Preservation:

☐ **Under what circumstances do you ever experience being "fearful" in any way?**

For example, name the most recent time you were afraid to try something - perhaps a new task or a different way of handling something you normally do one way and thought to try a different way. Or perhaps you were invited to go somewhere yet you did not go because you were fearful of something that might happen. What was that one thing? Be as specific as possible.

_____
_____
_____
_____
_____
_____
_____
_____
_____
_____
_____

Chapter 1 (Cont'd)

Relationships:

☐ **In what ways are you satisfied and happy with your relationships?** Where do you feel that relationships may be lacking intimacy or satisfaction, if any?

For example: Look at the current relationships in your life. Which one of them would you improve and in what way? What would you want to be different or better? Select at least one relationship in which you would want to increase your satisfaction or happiness. Describe it and how you would want to alter it.

_____

_____

_____

_____

_____

_____

Wealth & Finance:

☐ **How do you feel about your level of financial security or do you experience any lack of financial security?**
For example, in what particular case would you want to experience feeling more secure around money? Would it be in your daily expenses? In your current or future retirement account? In your ability to manage your finances or pay your bills? Be as specific as possible.

Chapter 1 (Cont'd)

_____

_____

_____

_____

_____

In any areas in which you experience dissatisfaction, describe them fully below...

_____

_____

_____

_____

_____

_____

_____

_____

_____

_____

_____

_____

_____

_____

Chapter 1 (Cont'd)

☐ **In your relationships?** Take some time to describe those feelings of dissatisfaction and where you can see that a relationship could be improved.

_____

_____

_____

_____

_____

_____

_____

_____

_____

_____

☐ **In your business, career or job?**
Take some time to describe here your experience and ways of feeling dissatisfaction with your business, career or job. **Note especially areas in which you are unsure about the source of that experience;** for example, why you feel the way that you do.

_____

_____

_____

_____

_____

Chapter 1 (Cont'd)

☐ **With regard to your present or future financial security?**
Describe here the specifics, to the best of your knowledge, and ways that you feel "stopped" or unable to move forward in achieving financial success or future security.

_____

_____

_____

_____

_____

☐ **With regard to fear or lack of security in areas other than finance?**
Describe your experience and ways you experience fear or worry about safety in life, outside the domain of money or finance. When have you ever felt fearful or unsure of your physical well-being and/or feared for your health?

_____

_____

_____

_____

_____

_____

Chapter 1 (Cont'd)

Where do you experience being limited in some way in your life?

_____

_____

_____

_____

_____

_____

_____

_____

_____

_____

Where do you feel that you stop yourself or do you feel that others stop you in experiencing success?

_____

_____

_____

_____

_____

_____

_____

_____

_____

Chapter 1 (Cont'd)

Last Question... Same area of inquiry:

Do you have an experience of lacking anything?

☐ Is it in the area of money or wealth?

☐ Is it in the area of self - esteem?

☐ Is it in the area of love?

☐ Do you receive the kind of recognition - at home or at work - that you yearn for?

Explain more fully here:

_____

_____

_____

_____

_____

_____

_____

_____

_____

It is, after all, your life - How will you know if you got what you came for if we don't get really specific about what it is you want?

Here now is an opportunity to reflect on your answers... Read what you wrote and answer the questions on the following page...

Chapter 1 (Cont'd)

In the area of Personal Relationships - What do you notice about what you wrote?

_____

_____

_____

_____

_____

_____

_____

_____

_____

_____

In the area of your Objectives to taking this program, what do YOU want to get out of it?

_____

_____

_____

_____

_____

_____

Chapter 1 (Cont'd)

_____

_____

_____

_____

_____

_____

_____

_____

_____

_____

_____

_____

_____

_____

_____

_____

_____

_____

_____

Great! Good work...

Now that you have completed that, move on to the next page.

Chapter 1 (Cont'd)

WHAT YOU WILL ACTUALLY GET: Now that you have looked at and explored what *you* think you want - let us tell you what we say you will get.

Here's what we have designed the program to deliver. Check it out - and then map it onto what YOU said you wanted. Is there a match? Is this something that will improve your current life? Remember, whether you get this, or not, is wholly dependent upon your active participation as you go through the program.

Promise of the Program

The Promise of this Program is that out of your successful completion of this program, you will **experience what is meant by "transformation" - a new access to personal power, a new view on financial prosperity, and a clear path to your next step as you create the life of your dreams.** You will experience a new perspective for living, such that you will have the tools that you need to experience a transformation in your life and your ability to act in ways that, right now, you cannot see are possible.

Your level of effective communications will exponentially expand, and you will see the areas of growth and development needed to accomplish what you want to create in your future...

Chapter 1 (Cont'd)

You will become clearer about what is stopping you in life and what is possible when you get past that. You will have the opportunity to break through what you think you are capable of doing and who you can be for yourself and for others.

This program will share with you some practical tools and distinctions that you can use regularly to keep pushing your self-imposed limits and create a **"paradigm shift"** in who you have known yourself to be. **In creating the future of your dreams, you will empower and serve others and create partnerships that benefit you and everyone you want to support.**

Let's look for a moment at what is meant by a **"Paradigm shift."**

So, paradigms are "frameworks" through which we see everything. We have many of them… and they limit the ways in which we interpret what we see through them. Paradigms can blind us from seeing something new because we are still looking at an experience through an old paradigm. For example, one old paradigm of telling time was that you had to have a timepiece with a little hand and a big hand and minutes were little lines and the two hands moved around the clock face to tell you what time it was.

That was how some "old timers" learned to tell time.

Chapter 1 (Cont'd)

Now, however, we have "digital" time, where numbers click by and tell us exactly what time it is to the second - or even millisecond - and we don't have to look at the round face of a clock at all. So why am I mentioning this? Well, in the 1980's when the Swiss watchmakers - who controlled the "timepiece" marketplace - were told about this newfangled way to tell time, **they completely disregarded it.** They said, "it's a fad, it won't work, it won't last" and they did not retool or even consider changing their view of manufacturing. They were looking at "telling time" through a particular **"paradigm."** The Japanese, however, were open to a new "paradigm" in timekeeping, and they had no investment in working with things "the old way," so they innovated, changed their view and a *new paradigm of timekeeping came into being.* They created a whole new industry around **digital time keeping** - and with that, Swiss watchmakers were left behind and had to play catch up with those who cornered the "timepiece" marketplace. **That is what discovering a "new paradigm" will do - it changes everything.**

One of the challenges of presenting a program like this without being face-to-face with you, Dear Student, is that I have no way of knowing what you already know and what you don't.

So, here's a request - and that is that you come to this program with something I would call a **"Beginner's Mind."**

Chapter 1 (Cont'd)

Here is what I mean by that.

I request that you engage with this material from a perspective that everything you learn here is new – not something you understand from the past. **Consider everything newly** and you will be amazed at the different perspectives that will show up inside that different "view." Be open to new "paradigms" of thinking. It is as if I am requesting that you look through a pair of binoculars; as you would view something perhaps in the far-off distance, bringing everything in your view "closer" to you. In a way, you will be examining everything newly - altering your viewpoint; seeing things differently. Literally, reframing your view of what you know to be "true." If you do this, we can promise you that a whole new world of possibilities will arise for you.

If you truly want to experience TRANSFORMATION; if you truly want to experience life differently; from a new perspective, you will have to do things in this program as it is designed – that is just the way this program works.

One more thing about the nature of this program.

Have you ever heard of the Law of Attraction? The best way I can describe it is that, like gravity, it is a natural law of the universe. You can't really see gravity at work... While it's true that you can see the

Chapter 1 (Cont'd)

results of it - like when you drop something, it falls to the ground. But you cannot actually SEE gravity, right?

Well, the Law of Attraction is, in theory, a natural law, like gravity. You cannot see it in operation; however, you can see the effect of it. For example, have you ever noticed that sometimes certain people appear to have a lot of bad luck? Sometimes it is called "bad karma?" Well, people who are supporters of the Law of Attraction would say that the reason they have bad luck is because of their attitude, **their way of being**, their negativity that "attracts" that kind of luck to them.

So, is that the truth?

Who can say. **Since you cannot SEE the Law of Attraction** in action, you can only make the assumption and then look at the evidence that follows. Take just a few moments to examine those times in your life when you have been particularly effective…

What was your attitude at the time? Were you looking forward to success? Were you anticipating good things? Proponents of the Law of Attraction would say that part of why you had "good things" come to you was because your attitude was one of positivity and clear intention rather than negativity and dwelling on what was not happening.

Chapter 1 (Cont'd)

We will revisit the Law of Attraction later on in the program... but for now, suffice it to say that having an awareness of it will impact your effectiveness as it relates to creating what you want in life.

That is where being open to new ways of thinking will impact the results of this book (program). We will be asking you to "take on" try on or adapt - even if temporarily - a new way of thinking about things. Consider, for example that you will attract what you dwell on in life. Good things - you attract good; bad things - you attract more bad. **All we ask is that you be willing to view life as a malleable thing and an amazing opportunity for new ways of thinking.**

Consider this with your beginner's mind: you may have the ability - through creating awareness - that you are more likely to attract what you want in your life when you consider that you **have the ability to do so.** That is an amazing opportunity and one that not everyone can see.

So, now, if you are clear that what we are promising is something you want in your life, you can continue reading. If not, you can give this book away as a gift to someone else who actually wants what we have to offer! **Either way you win!**

Let's look now at a new paradigm through a word we introduced to you already...

Chapter 1 (Cont'd)

ONTOLOGY

This is the second time you have heard this new word; so do you remember what it means?

Ontology is, as we said earlier, the study of "being" for human beings... and, as you move further into the "Book of Being," you will notice that we will be talking a lot about that word - "being" - and what it means as it relates to transformation and a transformational way of thinking and living.

For now, we are just going to delve a bit more into ontology - and what it means to you and your engagement in this program.

What follows here is an **"Ontological" conversation** about "ways of being" or human characteristics that we all share.
As far as we can tell, all human beings have several "human characteristics" regardless of where we come from. You could say they are the result of certain natural occurrences.
Try this on...

Early in my work with transformation, I was told that...

At about – best guess – 6 weeks of age - before you even have language to describe a feeling or a "thought" **something very powerful happens.**

Chapter 1 (Cont'd)

It occurs because up until then, generally speaking, a baby's every need is met. They wake up hungry, they get fed. They get wet, someone comes running and changes their diaper, they want to be held and comforted, someone is there to pick them up.

Then, 6 weeks or so into life... the first time they cry – and mom is busy or tired or napping, or just not willing to get up ONE more time that night...imagine the feeling of this coddled, pampered little human animal. Why, they are doing the same thing they have always done and ... **lo and behold... nothing happens!** They get worried – they get upset AND they experience a feeling that tells them – not in language because they don't have that yet – they get a FEELING that says – uh oh, "SOMETHING'S WRONG here!" **...and that's - (the theory goes) - where it all begins.** This feeling of invisible programming from the past - in the background every day of our lives after that... Can you see it?

Well, I used to believe that theory... However, now, after having given this some thought - and a good deal of study, **I have completely changed my mind!!**

I do not believe that is what actually what happened. NO... not at 6 weeks, or 3 weeks, or even 1 week!

Chapter 1 (Cont'd)

This experience - this "something is VERY wrong here"
phenomenon occurs - at BIRTH! (Let's pause here - for just a
second …Remember – what I said at the beginning of the book? –
This is not "The Truth" - Just try it on – and see if it works for you. It is
just one possible "view."

Okay, back to that moment of birth…

Think about it… Nine glorious months of floating in a warm,
cushioned, cozy environment… soft murmuring sounds, a weightless,
waterbed experience… when SUDDENLY - you, a new life - are
SQUEEZED into a tiny, tight shaft and thrust mercilessly into a
BRIGHT, loud, freezing COLD universe - and someone WHACKS you
on the behind! Welcome to the world!

…and your mind, your experience of life becomes in that moment
"Something is WRONG here!"

How could it be anything else?

That feeling, or decision you could call it, gets made at that very
moment - and for the **rest of your life you have this "feeling" that**
"something's wrong."

Chapter 1 (Cont'd)

That is what I'm referring to as a "Human Being characteristic" and one that's very much unconscious most of the time – **but it pretty much runs your life** – and mine - especially if we don't know it is there.

Think about it for a moment. What happens when things are really going well, what is usually your first thought "This can't last" - "I'm just waiting for the other shoe to drop" - "it's too good to be true." AND, when that phone call comes in the middle of the night - is your first thought "Oh, goodie - someone is calling with great news!" - NO! You just know it is something bad - because "something" is always wrong here!

So, we will be re-visiting these ontological conversations frequently throughout the course of this program… and one of the biggest opportunities of this work will be **identifying those unconscious thoughts or feelings** that are running the background that we don't even know are there but that get in the way of us feeling great and being truly happy in life.

Let me explain what I mean when I say, "running in the background…"

Chapter 1 (Cont'd)

You could compare it to a computer program. For example, Windows is a software program running in the background of your computer system. You can't see the program, you can only experience the result of having it. If you DIDN'T have it, all you would see is a black "dos" screen with a blinking cursor.

You actually see much more than that because you have an "invisible" program running in the background that allows you to actually see pictures and write things and interact on your computer in a completely natural way, right?

That is how your "unconscious programming" works as well. You can't see it, but it's there, running in the background, all the time.

Stay tuned for more "background conversations" to come!

The KEY!

Next, let's look at a subject that will be the key to your success in laying a powerful foundation for getting everything we just talked about. It is a new dimension - and a new distinction - for a common term - one that most of us have heard since we were children; mostly in the context of blame for what we did not do or say.

Chapter 1 (Cont'd)

Can you remember the first time someone - usually your parents - told you that you were not being "responsible?" - Possibly in connection with some household chore, or something similar that you were expected to do?

Well, what we are about to explore regarding that term - can literally alter life as you know it - IF - and ONLY IF, you are willing to experience the definition of that word in a whole new way.

We are going to "distinguish" being "responsible" as a place to come from - rather than as a reflection of something you are doing or not doing.

Please read the following definition **out loud** to yourself **twice ...slowly. Then, read it one more time.**

Consider what you hear as you read it... **No blame, no fault, without shame, credit or guilt.**

I have placed this definition on a page – by itself – so that, if you choose, you can copy it and paste it somewhere you can read it on a daily basis. It has proven to be an invaluable tool for me as I hope it will be for you. **Take it on and you will be amazed at the power it delivers in living a full and empowered life.**

Chapter 1 (Cont'd)

Definition of Responsibility

Responsibility starts with the willingness to experience your Self as cause... in the matter of your life.

Responsibility is not burden, fault, praise, blame, credit, shame or guilt. All these include judgments and evaluations of good and bad, right and wrong, or better and worse. They are not responsibility. They are derived from a ground of being in which the "Self" is considered to be a thing or an object rather than a context.

Responsibility starts with the willingness to deal with a situation from - and with the point of view, whether in the moment you realize it or not - that you are the source of what you are, what you do, and what you have. This point of view extends to include even what is done to you and, ultimately, what another does to another.

Responsibility ultimately is a context... for the source of what is.

(This definition is sourced by a quote of Werner Erhard)

Chapter 1 (Cont'd)

Before we explore this definition of responsibility further, I want to take just a moment to ask you if you are clear what we mean when we say **"Context?"**

I have found over the years that often people are unclear what that means and yet they are unclear that they are unclear! In other words, they assume they know what it means **when, in truth, they do not.**

So, let's take a moment to clear that up, shall we?

"The happiest people in the world are those who feel absolutely terrific about themselves, and this is the natural outgrowth of accepting total responsibility for every part of their life."

Brian Tracy

Chapter 1 (Cont'd)

I like to describe context and content this way: if you are looking at a clear glass of water in front of you, you could say **that the "glass" is the context** and the **water inside is the content.** So, what does that mean? Well, it means that the "context is decisive." By that I mean that the **context defines the form that the water (content) inside it takes.**

For example – if the glass is wide at the top and narrow at the bottom, the form that the water inside takes is? Right! **Wide at the top and narrow at the bottom**. If the glass is round rather than square, the water in the glass will take the "form" of **appearing "square," correct?**

Therefore, consider that the "context" for your life determines the "content." In other words, how you "view" your life (through what shape glass) will affect how life shows up for you. **How you view any situation** (once again, the shape of the glass) **will affect how that particular circumstance shows up for you.**

Now, back to "responsibility."

So, along with this "working" definition - **this new "view" of responsibility,** we are inviting you to consider that there are actually three levels; all included in the above definition.

Chapter 1 (Cont'd)

Before we define those three levels… **and identify where you are on that scale,** consider the following four questions as they relate to creating responsibility with no blame, guilt, shame or credit.

1. **Who is responsible for creating your world?** - As you ask yourself this question, consider that another way to say it is "Who creates my thoughts - in my head?"

    Your answer is "I do," right?

    > That's because your "world" - the one you create - awake or asleep - consciously or unconsciously - is behind your eyeballs - and the only one there is you, Ok. So, that brings us to the second question…

2. **Who can be in that world with me?"** - That is, who is IN your head - behind those same eyeballs - and that is…? **You,** and only you, correct?

    > You can explain, describe, and talk about "your view" or "your world" - AND no one else can really be "IN" it but you, right? Behind YOUR eyeballs…?

Chapter 1 (Cont'd)

3. **What happens to that world you are seeing through your eyeballs when you are gone -** die - or disappear?

   It disappears as well, right? Gone... it no longer exists?

So, consider this...

If you create your world, and no one else can be in it with you and it disappears when you are gone, **why would you *not* create a world that you loved?** Doesn't it make sense that you would create a world that was perfect for you and in which you could have whatever you wanted – **One where you were smart, beautiful, handsome, talented, etc.?** Since you can create it any way you want, every day is a new possibility for creating it the way you want it to be. There is only one catch.

You must be willing to see that you are at the source of everything you have in your life. This is where we ask you to look in defining the word "responsibility;" not whether you are right, wrong, good, or bad.

If you look 'in' your world – the one you've created in your head, you will see that **it IS possible for you to take responsibility for everything you have in your life**.

Chapter 1 (Cont'd)

Remember, when I say "responsible," I don't mean that you are at fault, or to blame, or even that you should be praised or acknowledged; **I mean ONLY that you caused what currently exists in your world; you caused everything.**

That means that YOU are truly "at cause" in the matter of your life. When you can acknowledge this, you are taking "responsibility" for your life and everything in it.

AND, you are clearly at Level 1 in the scale of responsibility!

Let's check it out here and see if it fits for you...

Levels of Responsibility
First Level: I am responsible for everything I do and see

As you saw from the four questions above, since you create YOUR world, you are responsible for everything that occurs in it!

You see your world or your universe through YOUR eyes.

You could say that what you see and what you do exists in your "thinking." Therefore, if you ask yourself "Who creates my world," you can see that it is you!

Chapter 1 (Cont'd)

If you look in your world – the one you have created in your head, **it is actually easy to see that you are responsible for everything you have in your life.** Remember, when we say "responsible," we do not mean that you are at fault, or to blame, or even that you should be praised or acknowledged; we mean ONLY that you are the source of what currently exists in your experience of your world.

That means that YOU are truly "at cause" in the matter of everything in your life. **When you can acknowledge this, you are taking "responsibility" for what you do and see in your life and along with responsibility comes power!**

Second Level: I am responsible for what others do to me and I do to them

The next level is that you are also "at cause" for everything that occurs in the lives of others in "your world." For example, when you think someone is being mean to you, you "cause" your experience of that. When someone around you is always ineffective, it exists in your world and you are a participant in it. **Consider the mom who always cleans up after her kids, but then complains about them not being dependable.** Remember, you create YOUR world, and you actually have a say in how it goes.

Chapter 1 (Cont'd)

Third and highest Level: I am responsible for what others to do others.

The final level of this "responsibility" is that you are also "at cause" for anything that occurs from the act of someone else on someone else. Once again, if it exists in YOUR world, you are "at cause" or the source.

Consider as well, from an energetic perspective; all of life is connected by energy and energy particles; therefore, anything I do impacts everything and everyone else on the planet; thereby I impact what others do and experience.

These three levels of "being responsible" have the possibility for providing you with great power – and the amount of power they give you is directly correlated to the level at which you get you as being "at cause" or at the source of everything.

You will see as you proceed through this program that **the more you can see what you created, the more you can impact your world** and the world around you. The more something exists outside of you, the less power you have.

Embrace responsibility; it is the source of your power.

Chapter 1 (Cont'd)

Let me use a story to demonstrate what I mean by that: Consider this scenario...

You are in your car, at an intersection, stopped for a red light. The car behind you plows into the back of your car. Under ordinary circumstances, who would you say is the person responsible for this accident? Given legalities (at least in the USA), the person in the car behind - who ran into the stopped car - would be the one to "blame." That is because under "ordinary circumstances," when we refer to someone as "responsible" we actually mean "to blame or "at fault." **We say they are wrong, or bad, etc.** However, this form of responsibility produces no power; it leaves you a victim of circumstance and exists merely to assign blame or guilt.

If we look at a more powerful view of "being responsible" - one that designates "owning" or "taking responsibility" as a way to empower someone as the "source" for what occurs in their life, we could consider this scenario differently. From the perspective of the person sitting at the light (and removing "blame" from the occurrence), **the person who is responsible for this accident is the person in the front car who is stopped at the light.**

Why would we say that? Because he or she put themselves there at that light at that moment in time. Therefore, they are the source for what occurred. **Not to blame** for what occurred but the

Chapter 1 (Cont'd)

source and, therefore, they have the power to choose where they are and when.

Please keep in mind this is not a matter of what is "true" or "untrue" - This is a matter of **creating a context** for living that empowers us - that has us be clear that WE create what we have and don't have by the choices we make - or don't make. It is not about truth - it is about languaging our lives in a way that has us own our choices and the consequences or rewards they bring. It is all part of conscious living; whether as individuals or as community members.

In other words, we can blame others - which gives us no power to change anything (since most of us know that the only person we can change is us) or we can take responsibility for whatever has occurred and then make different choices.

This is what gives us the power in our own lives and in making a difference in the world. This is the first step to transforming our view of the world and our place in it.

Take a moment here to reflect on what we have just covered. Make notes here about what you notice in your thinking about "responsibility" and at what level you believe you find yourself at this moment.

Chapter 1 (Cont'd)

_____

_____

_____

_____

_____

_____

_____

_____

_____

_____

Now it's time to provide your AffirmActions & Assignment for Empowerment Chapter 1 - Turn to the next page.

Chapter 1 (Cont'd)

Understanding and engaging in AffirmActions

AffirmAction: Working Definition

> **"Affirmation"** is an intellectual process: Something affirmed or declared to be true...It is an internal, positive statement or judgment; a self-declaration that does not necessarily change anything in the real world.

> **"Action"** is an act taken or a thing done.

> **"AffirmAction"** **is a combined process:** It provides evidence in the real world of an intellectual, internal, self-declaration.

Descriptors:

- **AffirmAction** is an experiential affirming **behavior** demonstrating **in the real world** a positive change or outcome of a created possibility
- **AffirmAction** takes an idea or internal concept and makes it real or brings it into reality
- An **AffirmAction** is a **realized affirmation caused by one's taking action** to make it so
- **AffirmAction** is an affirmation made real by a **consciously committed action**

CHAPTER 1 - AFFIRMACTION #1

1. This week, consider one area of your life in which you can see a particular paradigm that has influenced or "colored" your way of thinking.

   Here is one example of how your week would look if the paradigm you took on was as follows:

   Let's pretend that you are someone whose parents always told them that **"You must work hard to make money, and no one will give you anything."** You would then assume and be influenced by that statement. Therefore, **unless you were working hard,** you would have no expectation that you would ever be able to have money. You would have created **the paradigm of "scarcity" and that money and good things are hard to come by.** Now, let's say you shifted that paradigm to one of **"Money comes to me easily and I am always the object of generosity"**- would your life be any different? The answer is yes (*in case you didn't get that yet*)!

   AFFIRM: So, taking that example to the next step, you would next change your internal conversation about **wealth** and to do that, would **create an action that creates and solidifies that new paradigm.**

THE BOOK OF BEING...

Chapter 1 (Cont'd)

Every day, you could begin to **look for examples and cases where money comes easily, and people are generous to you and to others.** You could start each day by repeating to yourself - as you would an affirmation - **"Money comes to me easily and I am always the object of generosity."**

ACTION: Finally, each day, you could make sure you are **generous with those around you;** notice where others are generous and authentically acknowledge that to them. Give generously of yourself to others and, when appropriate give away or donate something to someone in need.

Begin to look for evidence that life is bountiful, that you don't always have to work hard to gain benefits and that money can come easily and effortlessly to you. Take note at the end of each day of any changes you notice in yourself and in the world around you. **Where is your new paradigm showing up?**

Each day, write down at the end of each Chapter (We will be leaving space for that in this Playbook) or in your journal, the paradigm you are at work on and how is your "shift in thinking" going?

CHAPTER 1 ASSIGNMENT

Continue this experiment until you begin to experience a shift in your way of seeing life in this area. **Then take on another!**

You can start here!

_____

_____

_____

_____

_____

_____

_____

_____

_____

_____

_____

_____

_____

_____

_____

_____

_____

_____

_____

_____

EMPOWERMENT CHAPTER 2

What Does "Transformation" Mean - REALLY?

Before we can go any further in this "Book of Being," we need to take a moment to describe "transformation" so let's jump in there.

In Chapter 1, we frequently mentioned the word "transformation." What exactly do we mean by that?

Is transformation change? Is it exchanging one way of "being" for another? While transformation as a definition can be difficult to describe - it is amazing to experience. It can happen in a moment or can happen over years.

While it is commonly and interchangeably used to describe a "change" of experience in life, it is very distinct from change. Transformation carries nothing of the past with it, whereas change always does. Transformation is a fundamental alteration in the way that reality or life shows up in one's view. It is as if you are accustomed to viewing life from one perspective and suddenly, something, someone or even life itself (or a view of life) occurs in a completely different way, impacting everything else.

Chapter 2 (Cont'd)

For example, telling time digitally was a transformation in the way we viewed the act of measuring time - not because it appeared digitally, but because neither gears, nor hands, nor anything else about telling time remained the same and a whole new view of life emerged because the experience of "digital" occurred.

Philosophers, writers, and thinkers have been talking about enlightenment and transformation for thousands of years – and are we truly any clearer about what that means today?

Transformation exists in the world of "being" – of that much we are certain. To be transformed is a way that one experiences life and the lives of others around them. It has little import in the world of doing.

So, if we're going to explore this human "being" conversation and transformation and how they relate, we need to go back to the original conversation we had in Empowerment Chapter 1 when I introduced you to ontology, the being of human beings.

Ontologically speaking... as human beings, we all have something ...some old conversations in our head from our past, that colors our present – It literally colors who we know ourselves to be and how we think of ourselves in life.

Chapter 2 (Cont'd)

Take a moment and write the following: If I was describing myself – as a stranger – to myself, what - or more accurately – who would I say I am - as an individual? (do not turn the page until you complete writing this down.

_____

_____

_____

_____

_____

_____

_____

_____

_____

_____

_____

_____

_____

_____

_____

_____

_____

_____

_____

_____

Chapter 2 (Cont'd)

So, let's see. What did you say? How did you describe yourself? A really nice person – Smart? Incredibly creative? Loving? An unselfish friend? A gifted learner? Beloved by all who know me? Capable of making a difference in the world?

My guess is that if you are like most of us, probably not.

Theoretically then, it would follow, that for most of us, we exist for ourselves as someone who is usually "less than..." You know what I mean – Less smart than I think I should be, right? Less pretty than I should be? More timid (or loud) than I think I should be? Certainly, less confident than I should be? And definitely fatter, thinner, stronger, or less fit than I think I should be...

Does any of this sound familiar to you – any of it at all?

By the way, I guess you could be that "one in a million" individual who doesn't have those thoughts about yourself, but I doubt it or you probably wouldn't have bought this book! I would even venture to say you would not really exist in the real world, because, ontologically speaking, according to our theory, all of the above are traits of being human – and you are human, right?

We all have our own version of these thoughts about ourselves – and, they are not personal. **More about that in a minute.**

Chapter 2 (Cont'd)

Now, admitting that I see these things about myself (or yourself) does not make me unique... nor does it transform me in any way...

What it could do, however, is awaken an awareness in me that I, and you, and all of us, have these internal, disempowering conversations about ourselves – unconscious for the most part – running in the background of our consciousness... undermining our confidence and frequently keeping us "stuck."

Now, what could make us unique? What could, literally, transform who we are in the world is to become more conscious – really awake – to the fact that we have these thoughts about ourselves and that these "thoughts" are not who we are.

Now, back to a statement I made three paragraphs up – **that these thoughts are not personal.**

They are not personal because we all have them –different versions, same tune.

That is because these "thoughts" are not "YOU" thinking; they are brain reactions – merely electronic impulses – brain reactions to incidents, statements made by others which have been misunderstood or misinterpreted, stories our childhood brains recorded and stored for future reference...all seemingly "true" when our brains recorded them.

Chapter 2 (Cont'd)

That is because our brain is very much a non-discriminating recording device, and, like an mp3 player, the gathered information is played back to us each and every moment of our day – especially when we are most stressed, confronted or challenged by the unknown or something with which we are unfamiliar.

Why is that?

Well, let's look at that next.

Here are some scientific facts that impact your ontological and physiological behavior…

All human brains – (**see science reference material at the end of the book if you want more technical research to back this up) – have something called a Reptilian component. It is related to the Limbic brain, which is responsible for emotions and value judgments based on emotions and is closely related and influenced by the Reptilian or "survival" brain as it is called.

These brain parts do not operate independently of one another. They have numerous interconnections through which they influence one another, and they have a strong influence on your reactions and the choices you unconsciously make in your life.

Chapter 2 (Cont'd)

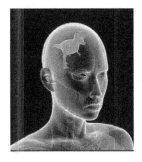

Early man: The survival brain was essential to preserve life in early man because quick reactions (flight or fight) were required for survival of the species.

Modern man: The survival brain is no longer essential to preserve life; we have changed our environment and our living conditions such that we are able to consciously preserve life and, for the most part, in daily living, unless we are standing in the middle of the street and do not see the bus coming, we do not need these "automatic" responses to the degree that primitive man did. **However, and this is a big however...**

The primitive brain still exists – and is programmed to connect with our **emotions** – through which it controls its "perceived" method of survival. This perceived method of survival is ...are you ready for this? This is a monumental statement.

The Survival brain is programmed to always, always, be right! Being right is its method of surviving.

Being right that the saber tooth tiger will not be outside the cave to eat me - being right about the tribe that is encroaching on my territory, being right about that I have to save the last drop of water for myself or I will die.

Chapter 2 (Cont'd)

Response to a chemical binary code - we are the machine... the brain machinery...

When you can disassociate yourself from the machine - the limbic brain - the automatic way of reacting that runs our life - only then do we become who we truly are...

THAT is transformation!

Now, this information could leave you in a couple of different places... confused, concerned, enlightened, in the dark and wondering why you even started this program in the first place. Well, any place you are is perfect. Your "mechanics" are merely trying to figure it all out. And that is very natural so wherever you are right now is fine!

Now that you are clear about what we are talking about when we say this is a transformational program about being, **you will be clearer to what we are referring, right?**

Now let's move on to your assignment for Chapter 2 and its associated AffirmActions...

You know the ones you promised would do!! Onward, brave warrior for transformation, onward!

Chapter 2 (Cont'd)

Bad things happen. And the human brain is especially adept at making sure that we keep track of these events. This is an adaptive mechanism important for survival.

David Perlmutter

Chapter 2 (Cont'd)

CHAPTER 2 – AFFIRMACTIONS & ASSIGNMENT

1. **When you awake, notice the conversation inside your head that you awake to.** Notice the thoughts and notice who is thinking those thoughts. Are they empowering or disempowering thoughts? Write them down here…

   _____

   _____

   _____

   _____

   _____

   _____

   _____

   _____

   _____

   _____

   _____

2. **Notice the background "mood" behind those thoughts.** Are you anxious to jump out of bed and get started with your day or are you noticing a reluctance to leave the warmth of your blankets and comfort of your pillow. If you could wake up into a different thought, what would it be? Write that down.

Chapter 2 (Cont'd)

_____
_____
_____
_____
_____
_____
_____
_____
_____
_____
_____
_____
_____

"You want to become aware of your thoughts and choose your thoughts carefully because you are the masterpiece of your own life."

Joe Vitale

Chapter 2 (Cont'd)

AFFIRM: Take some time tomorrow morning to **create an empowering thought for the day**. Create a statement or an affirmation to live by - just for one day. It can be anything - any thought you would love to have. **Today will be ...?**

Some suggestions: Amazing! Exciting! Empowering? Energizing? Successful? Full of Energy? Satisfying...Fulfilling!

_____

_____

_____

_____

_____

_____

Take your pick! Take on any of these "ways of being." Something other than the ordinary thoughts you wake up into most days. You may not feel it right away - that's ok. And, that little voice in your head will be arguing about how impractical or foolish or whatever it tells any of us so that you may experience feeling foolish or like you are wasting your time. You're not! That is just the past pulling for what is familiar.

Give it some time - and continue re-programming your limbic brain. Say that new, created thought to yourself at least 15 times.

Chapter 2 (Cont'd)

ACTION: Next, get into action to make it so! What would your life look like if today were *Amazing*! or Fulfilling! or Full of Energy? What would you be wearing? Put it on! What would you be eating for breakfast - do it! What would you be saying? Begin to say those things and create your satisfying, fulfilling day! Notice what changes and notice your experience of living a created day instead of the one you "automatically" woke up into this morning.

Tonight, write down here or in your journal how it went - what worked, what didn't work - and tomorrow, create another way of being - another thought that makes it worth your time to get up in the morning.

_____

_____

_____

_____

_____

_____

_____

_____

_____

_____

Do this every day this week.

Chapter 2 (Cont'd)

"The best way to predict the future is to invent it."

Steve Jobs

"Neither a wise man nor a brave man lies down on the tracks of history to wait for the train of the future to run over him."

Dwight D. Eisenhower

EMPOWERMENT CHAPTER 3

Consciously Reframe Your Communications

"Mean What You Say, Say What You Mean,

Don't say it Mean & and Clean it up If You Do!"

Well, Dear Reader, you have survived Chapter 2 – and you are still here - Good work!

How did your assignment go? Did you find it difficult or easy? Take some notes to yourself here or in your notebook.

_____

_____

_____

_____

_____

_____

_____

_____

_____

_____

_____

Chapter 3 (Cont'd)

What did you learn from Chapter 2? Write that down.

_____

_____

_____

_____

_____

_____

_____

_____

_____

_____

_____

_____

_____

_____

_____

_____

_____

_____

_____

_____

_____

_____

_____

_____

_____

Chapter 3 (Cont'd)

_____

_____

_____

_____

_____

_____

_____

_____

_____

_____

As you recently explored ontology, the mind, the limbic brain, etc., you could be really experiencing thinking overload! It's a lot to handle, isn't it?

Well, guess what – more to come! We're going to do a quick review on what we learned about your new concept of Responsibility...

So, with your beginner's mind, at what level can you honestly say you find yourself now?

Level 1 – I am responsible for everything I do.

>   Actually, if you cannot say you have reached at least this level, I am not sure there is any purpose in you continuing to read further.

THE BOOK OF BEING...

Chapter 3 (Cont'd)

As we see it, you have three choices; Either give this book to someone who is committed to experience transformation, come back when you are serious about engaging in the Book of Being, or start over from the Introduction.

Level 2 – I am responsible for everything I do and for everything others do to me.

> *This is a huge leap forward – if you can honestly embrace being at this level – even for short periods – you are doing well. Congratulations!! Continue reading…*

Level 3 – I am responsible for everything I do, everything others do to me, and everything others do to others.

> *If you can truly say you find yourself embracing this level – even from time to time – the rest of this program will be a breeze for you!*

If you take the case that you are at level 2 of responsibility, then you can see that how you impact others by what you say and how you say it is the source for how you are responsible for what others do to you.

Let's explore that a bit more.

Chapter 3 (Cont'd)

Consider this... Just try it on- as you would a new coat or dress. See how it fits... practice thinking of this concept... Consider that it isn't necessarily the truth – as nothing we will be telling you in this "Book" is the "truth."

This is a theory that, when experienced can make a difference for you – you, the human being who wants to experience all that is possible in the domain of being human - a real transformation in how you are currently living; which is largely reaction and survival.

Ok. Here it goes.

Everything we do in life depends upon our skill level at communication. How can you see that it would be valuable to improve in that area?

I am going to give you something here that could be very helpful to you in the area of communication, especially when communicating with more than one person at a time. It is a communication based on a distinction created b**y Peter Senge in his book titled "The Fifth Discipline,"** an excellent read, by the way.

Please take the time - before you go further into the program - to read the following pages on the distinction between Dialogue and Discussion. I assure you that you will make good use of it in times ahead (and probably see where it would have been useful to have read it in difficult times past!).

Chapter 3 (Cont'd)

NOTES ON DIALOGUE / DISCUSSION

"She had played games before. Winning had been everything and showing her own prowess meant she was important and valued; but this was different, bigger somehow. Being on the basketball court and looking for the opening that was going to make the most difference for the team, instead of going for her own "Glory shot" - that was a different feeling. "Exhilarating," just about said it all.

For years, the coach had been talking to them about synergy and the whole being greater than each of their separate power plays. She missed it until now - and she knew as she stood there, that the results produced on the scoreboard that night were far bigger than a game won. It was a collective gathering of skills and knowledge. Together the team was unbeatable, because, win or lose the game, they were all winners."

In ping-pong, tennis and racquetball, the speed and power of the game can rivet your attention and present you with a momentary excitement. However, when you watch a championship team play basketball, football or soccer, you witness synergy in action. Synergy - the poetry of men and women working together, each adding his or her special individual skill to create synergy, the whole bigger than the separate parts... And, so it is with dialogue and discussion; two primary types of communication; each with a different purpose.

Chapter 3 (Cont'd)

Both are important and can produce worthwhile results; however, the synergy that occurs when both are used becomes evident when the distinction between them is clear for everyone. You could examine this phenomenon further through looking at the roots of the two words.

DISCUSSION: Its root is the same as percussion and concussion. It suggests something like a verbal ping-pong game, where we hit the subject back and forth between us. In such a game, the subject of common interest is taken apart or analyzed by many points of view provided by the participants. This can be useful, of course.
Yet the purpose of the game is to win; meaning one person's views are accepted by the group as the "right ones" or the road that must be taken.

DIALOGUE: The roots of the word dialogue are "moving through "-free flow of meaning between people; as a stream flows between two banks. That stream, accessed through dialogue, could be called a collective thinking space -- space made up of thoughts floating on the surface of that stream of common knowledge and gathered in by those along the banks; to be examined with appreciation for the differences as much as the similarities they bring. People can participate in a pool of common thinking created by this "everyman's stream." Through dialogue, people can access the bigger possibility available when they are open to gaining from everyone's contribution.

Chapter 3 (Cont'd)

An egg yolk, when fried on a griddle, shows up like a yellow circle --
single and alone.   When mixed in a cake, its individual characteristics
are invisible, yet this essential ingredient provides something that
expands the value of the whole.

Similarly, it's like transforming five or six individual ingredients into a
cake, exponentially altering the ultimate result. The total sum of its
parts is far greater than the individual characteristics. For this pool of
common knowledge to be most effectively accessed through dialogue
three basic conditions are necessary:

1. All participants must suspend their assumptions; literally hold them
   as if suspended above the conversation.
2. All participants must regard one another as colleagues.
3. There must be a facilitator who supports the context of dialogue.

To suspend one's assumptions and opinions means to acknowledge
that you have them and yet be able to put them aside for the period of
the dialogue. It must be understood that everyone will still have their
opinions which, during the course of dialogue, will be suspended. The
intent is to give all possible ideas the opportunity to be heard,
considered, and valued.

Chapter 3 (Cont'd)

In dialogue, everyone is a colleague. People feel that they are building something together that could not be designed separately or alone. Defensiveness is put aside, and a facilitator can assist in maintaining the context of dialogue. He or she does this by walking a careful line between being helpful in the process at hand and by asking participants to distinguish whether they are in dialogue or discussion. Even when people share a common vision, they may have different ideas about how to achieve it.

Dialogue allows for the free flow of conflicting ideas. Such creative inquiry is what allows a new solution to be discovered -- solutions that no individual could have seen. Just as personal vision provides a foundation for building a shared vision, reflection and inquiry skills provides a foundation for dialogue and discussion.

Both dialogue and discussion can lead to new courses of action. In a discussion, different views are presented and defended, and this may provide a useful analysis of the whole situation. In a dialogue, different views are presented as a means of discovering a totally new view.

While the dialogue produced when individuals share their insights and ideas generates the kind of powerful thinking that can change the course of history, discussion can be an important contribution in group decision-making.

Chapter 3 (Cont'd)

THEORY

There are primarily two distinctions in verbal communications. When people are engaged in dialogue, they expand their views and can access a larger pool of knowledge. When discussion is used, communication focuses in and decisions are made.

PREDICTION

A combination of dialogue and discussion is the most effective means of continual generative learning. The power lies in their synergy and in being able to distinguish between them.

Sourced by Peter Senge in "The Fifth Discipline"

Was this useful?

You may want to jot down here some thoughts you may have had while reading this piece on Dialogue and Discussion.

_____

_____

_____

_____

_____

Chapter 3 (Cont'd)

_____

_____

_____

_____

_____

_____

Can you think of some times in the past when you can see this "distinction" would have been useful for you? In other words, can you think of a recent time when you experienced being in a "discussion" rather than a dialogue when a dialogue was what was needed? Describe that instance here…

_____

_____

_____

_____

_____

_____

_____

_____

_____

_____

_____

Chapter 3 (Cont'd)

Chapter 3 (Cont'd)

As we continue to delve into the subject of communication, a great question to contemplate is "What constitutes communication? What are the different parts?" Here's a hint – there are three of them...
The answer is...

- **Words**
- **Voice tone, and**
- **Body language**

And what value, in percentage, does each of these play in effective communication?

Experts tell us **voice tone is 38%, Body language is 55% and Words...? Those all-important** words that we think are so important - are merely 7% of the message!

Is that surprising?

I know it surprised the heck out of me when I heard it almost 20 years ago.

Try this experiment: Using only the following words, "There is plenty of time," convey to a friend the following emotions... anger, frustration, joy, satisfaction, sadness, or concern. **See if they can tell what emotion you are feeling.** It is likely that they will interpret or misunderstand YOUR emotion based on how THEY would display that emotion, rather than what you are attempting to communicate.

Chapter 3 (Cont'd)

Consider, if you will - demonstrated by the exercise you just did - the potential for damage you and I can do if we rely strictly on a method of communication like email... Why do you think that is the case? Have YOU ever had an email misunderstood? Misinterpreted?

Well, that's because email only conveys **7% of the message to the "receiver".**

I can tell you, after working in this field for years, it's true. Remember, in the previous exercise, you only had five words, **"There is plenty of time,"** and yet we were able to express a lot of emotion behind them.

If you think about those numbers and then about email, texting, tweeting, etc., you can see that all – in business as well as personally - have the potential to be at the source of many problems.
You can see that, because two of the three areas of communication are missing – when all there is are the words – **93% of the message!**

All the rest gets "filled in" by the receiver! AND what they fill in is constituted from their own "filters" about what you said AND what they think you meant by what you said.

What do you think I mean by **"filters**?"

Chapter 3 (Cont'd)

That will require an ontological conversation - and one which we will get to very soon. First, though, **let me explain a little bit more about the perspectives of communication...**

We could say there are two languaging perspectives in communicating – listening and speaking or receiving a message (listening) or sending a message (speaking).

In receiving a message, or listening (as we normally call it), you may notice that, when listening to someone, it sometimes it feels like you need to respond in some way - to comment or say something in response to the person speaking so that they understand that you actually ARE listening. Really, though, what I have found through the years, is that if I am truly listening to what someone is saying, **they will know it by who I am authentically "being"** and, if I am with them in person, by my open or closed body language including what level of eye contact I am making with them (much more about this "being" to come!! It is, after all, part of the title of this program!).

Let's take some time here to really explore the phenomenon of "listening" or receiving a message or communication.

Chapter 3 (Cont'd)

Remember to stay in touch with your "beginner's mind…"

Listening (Receiving)

Ok - time now for that ontological conversation about "filters."

The kind of "filter" we are referring to is a language filter; that something that colors or influences everything that is seen "through" it. For example, yellow sunglasses.

Have you ever tried on a pair of yellow sunglasses?

They are designed to cut out the ultraviolet rays of the sun so that only certain "rays" pass through to your eyes. Those "filters" literally color the world you see in front of you. When you first put them on everything looks yellow. Then, once you wear them for a while - even a few minutes - everything starts to look normal and you no longer can tell you are wearing those "yellow" glasses. UNTIL you take them off - then your eyes adjust and the real colors emerge.

That kind of filter occurs in the human mind and it is through that kind of filter that you hear everything.

That filter is an ontological phenomenon caused by a "survival" mechanism and it colors everything you see and hear.

As a matter of fact, our "listening" could be said to be made up of everything we have ever heard or   learned…

Chapter 3 (Cont'd)

AND, we've heard a LOT and everything we see and hear now is filtered through that "past based" mind.

So, consider what we talked about earlier – in our Chapter on Ontology and the human brain... [Chapter 2 page 72]

If you recall, we said that your brain, for the most part, spends its time assuring the survival of the "thing" it perceives as "you." **It is a reaction-based mechanism and, by its very nature, is based on what it knows to be "true."** So, taking into consideration that there are an enormous number of memories it can choose from to justify survival, being right and the truth about life, these past thoughts, feelings and experiences could be said to be "always present" in your unconscious mind, and you hear everything in life through these "filters" from the past.

Let me give you an example.

You are 7 years old and your grandparents are coming to dinner. **Your mother reminds you that "your grandparents are old and they do not like a lot of noise.** You know you sometimes can get noisy so remember to be quiet when they are around. **Speak only when you are spoken to and do not volunteer any additional information, understand?** Especially, don't tell them about your award at school because they will think you are bragging and bragging is not nice. I will tell them all about it, don't worry."

Chapter 3 (Cont'd)

You follow your mother's instructions, stay in the background, make little noise, **speak only when spoken to** and wait for your mother to tell your grandparents about your award at school. It never happens.

After your grandparents leave, you ask your mom why she did not tell them and she says, **"Oh honey, they were busy and we were all occupied with catching up on our lives. We'll mention it next time, ok?"**

So, let's look at this brief encounter. There were several opportunities for this young, impressionable mind to formulate some pretty strong "filters" or, you could say, limiting beliefs about themselves and about others. **Can you identify one?**

Without reading further, jot down some of your ideas below. Then, turn the page and see what you may have missed.

_____

_____

_____

_____

_____

_____

_____

_____

Chapter 3 (Cont'd)

_____
_____
_____
_____
_____
_____
_____
_____
_____
_____
_____
_____
_____
_____
_____
_____
_____
_____
_____
_____
_____
_____
_____
_____

Chapter 3 (Cont'd)

Let's look at them together…

1) Older people do not like a lot of noise. Can you see where this could be "limiting" for you and for any older person you encounter later in your life? Did you think of that one? Take a moment to give that some thought right now. Would that be likely to impact your behavior around older people? Your opinions about older people?

2) Speak only when you are spoken to. How many of us can relate to "keeping our mouths shut" unless we are asked to speak? Children who are not encouraged to speak up for themselves can easily be "shut down" as adults. Do you know anyone like that? Someone who is afraid to speak up for what they want; who spends time hoping they will be heard but are unwilling to take a stand for what they want or even to ask for what they deserve?

3) What about the promise that was made "I'll tell them about your award." Broken promises yield an experience of distrust. How many people do you know who find it difficult to trust others? Is that something with which you have difficulty? While trust of others begins with trusting ourselves, it is not uncommon to find that children who have been lied to or who have been deceived as youngsters find it difficult to trust others as adults.

4) Bragging is not nice. Do you know someone who finds it difficult to accept a complement? Is that something YOU experience?

Chapter 3 (Cont'd)

Do you deflect or minimize someone's acknowledgements of you? Why would you do that? Perhaps, because you – like so many of us as children - were warned that "it's not nice to think too highly of yourself or others will think you are bragging." Appreciating your own competence and allowing someone else's acknowledgment to contribute to you, is actually a gift – to them. Have you ever attempted to acknowledge someone, only to have them deflect or deny their worth? As the extender of the complement, it can actually be quite frustrating and quite a letdown when you want to acknowledge someone who cannot seem to let it in. Remember that the next time someone wants to say something nice about you. Let it in – and thank them for the experience.

Believe it or not, letting someone's acknowledgement in is a bigger gift to them than it is to you **(That could be one of those "stranger than fiction" facts about being human)!**

These kinds of filters – and limiting beliefs – are present for all of us and, as you can imagine, they impact everything we hear and every conversation we have. It colors our thinking, and, most especially our listening; that is what others say to us.

Here's what I mean.

Consider that, rarely do we actually hear what other people are saying to us.

Chapter 3 (Cont'd)

Consider that what we hear is our interpretation of what they are saying; what we think they mean by what they are saying. We listen to what they are saying through the filters in our mind that distort their message to fit something we have heard or believed from the past.

So now, consider this. Those conversations from the past - our past - influence everything that we hear in the present - unless we are aware and awake to that happening. Only then can we choose something other than those automatic interpretations. Let me remind you that these interpretations and beliefs from the past are called "limiting beliefs," because that is exactly what they do; they limit us; our behavior, our understanding of others, and our ability to create our lives moment to moment.

They limit our way of thinking, of listening, of living in the moment - and keep us from truly being present. Being present in a way that we can truly hear what others are actually saying rather **than our interpretation of what others are saying** or what others *mean* by what they are saying. Imagine, the difference that is possible when you are able to just listen to someone; without the filters, without the interpretations and without the limiting beliefs from the past.

Just being with someone and listening, with an open mind and an open heart, can make all the difference in the world when someone is upset or looking for support.

THE BOOK OF BEING...

Chapter 3 (Cont'd)

Most of the time, they do not want answers or advice. How you know is – and this is the key **- they don't ask for it**. What most of us do when someone has a problem is –what? That's right – we want to fix it or change it or give them the solution.

A critical piece of being a good listener is to JUST LISTEN. If someone wants advice, usually they'll ask. The other option is ASK if they want any feedback or coaching or if they just want to talk about what's bothering them. They will tell you whether they are open to hearing what you have to say.

It's really important to be with them and not be looking for the "answer." This is important because YOUR answer may not be the right one for them.

Another thing to keep in mind is that *your* mind actually works at lightning speed – a lot faster than the speaker's tongue in many cases. That is why, many times we are way "ahead" - making up the end of the speaker's sentence before it is even out of their mouth. We even already have the answer for them! A good tool to use to counteract that, if you are committed to being a good listener, is to repeat to yourself what they said. **This keeps your attention from wandering and from interrupting before they are finished.**

What's not in the words - One more thing can be said about listening:

Chapter 3 (Cont'd)

Sometimes what is most important about a conversation is in **what is not said.** Truly, it could be said that "how" you listen to another person, gives them power.

For example, have you ever been with someone who listens to you like you are a loser? As someone who makes mistakes? As someone who is awkward? Perhaps in school or by thoughtless friends or associates?

I have and how I felt afterwards, even if they NEVER said a WORD to me, my experience was that they thought I was stupid and what I had to say had no value. I have also been with people who "listened" me as powerful, intelligent, and well worth listening to. Amazingly, that is exactly how I showed up in the world after being with those kinds of listeners. **They are the kind of listeners who make a difference in the world –** just by "being" there for someone else – you could say for "taking a stand" for someone else's greatness.

As you go through this week, instead of worrying about what you are saying (as most of us usually are) - and how you are saying it, I invite you to stay present to your listening for others. Ask yourself this...**What is the "listening" I am bringing to every conversation?**

What interpretations am I making about what this person is saying? Am I truly listening to them and being there for them?

Chapter 3 (Cont'd)

Remain conscious of when you are and **are not** actively listening to what someone else is saying and doing that alters your perception of what is happening around you.

More than you know, **you are actually creating your environment and your reactions to those around you and the conversations in which you participate truly influence the outcome of nearly everything in your life and in the lives of others.**

What follows on the next page are some useful notes on the powers of listening…

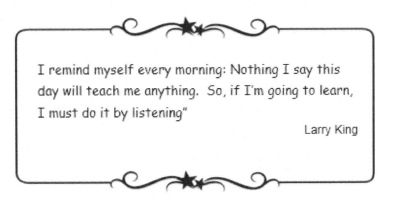

I remind myself every morning: Nothing I say this day will teach me anything. So, if I'm going to learn, I must do it by listening"

Larry King

Chapter 3 (Cont'd)

NOTES ON LISTENING SKILLS

Consider the qualities of a "Good Listener..."

- Non-judgmental
- Make eye contact
- Refrain from interrupting
- Empathetic
- Caring
- Present

Consider the challenges of a "Poor Listener." They could be experiencing...

<u>Internal distractions like...</u>

- ✓ Physical discomfort or illness
- ✓ Tired, disinterested, bored, have personal problems
- ✓ Attitude
- ✓ Hearing problems
- ✓ Daydreaming

<u>External distractions</u>

- ✓ Noise
- ✓ Weather (good or bad)
- ✓ Music
- ✓ Disruptions
- ✓ Co-workers or friends interrupting

Chapter 3 (Cont'd)

Given this information, finding good listeners is a rare commodity!
Look at all the things we must overcome to develop this skill!

How to Improve YOUR Listening Skills…

It is not always a "personal issue" that causes poor listening.

Because the human mind processes incoming information nearly five times faster than the words can be registered by the listener, people tend to "jump ahead" or make assumptions (as if they already know what someone is saying before they say it) long before someone finishes a sentence. To counter those "human" conditions, here are some tips for improving everyone's listening skills:

- **Mentally summarize** – Sometimes it helps to repeat to yourself what you have already heard so that you can stay in touch with the "present" conversation
- **Make eye contact and stay focused** on the person in front of you
- **Put yourself in the other person's place**
- **Practice, practice, practice**

Be aware that each of us has the ability to "listen" someone a certain way…

Chapter 3 (Cont'd)

Powerful Listening

Can you think of a time when you spoke to a teacher or a mentor or someone **who had confidence in you and in your abilities?** That means they showed you the kind of respect and attention that empowered your speaking and had you feel good about who you were, how you were communicating, and what you had to offer in what you were saying.

Their "way of listening" to you and being with you, was empowering and in being that way with you, they created a **"listening"** of you for others that was powerful. The result was you feeling more self-confident and able.

You could say they listened *FOR* your greatness, rather than your limitations. Make note here of someone who, because of the way they "listened *for*" the greatness in you, they empowered you.

_____

_____

_____

_____

_____

Also, all of us, at one time or another, have had someone do the opposite or someone who had us feel that nothing we said was right or who "disempowered" us by the way they listened to us. I invite you to resolve to refrain from ever doing that to someone else.

Chapter 3 (Cont'd)

Remember, **powerful listening can create possibility, or it can shut it down!**

I invite you to be a positive, **powerful, listener** *for the greatness in others!*

Now let's shift our view for a moment to the "speaking" side of communication...

Powerful Speaking

If you are the person speaking, always consider your message and who will receive it.

My experience is that as a speaker, **mostly we want to make sure people hear what WE have to say.** Little regard is given to speaking to the other person's "listening."

That means **considering their filters, their beliefs, their stories, and speaking in such a way that they actually have an interest in hearing** what you have to say. That means speaking in a way that leaves them empowered and interested, rather than offended or disinterested.

Consider for a moment how effective you will be when addressing someone else's concerns, rather than assuming that yours are the most important.

Chapter 3 (Cont'd)

Learning about what touches, moves and inspires others can open up all sorts of possibilities for you and for them.

Life is pretty simple once you see that you will win at the game of life when others win at theirs. The universe just moves with more velocity that way.

Finally, as a speaker, authenticity and talking "straight" is the source and the beginning of everything powerful.

For example, have you ever wanted to say "no" to something but said "yes" instead because it was easier? You may have justified this by thinking you could get out of it at a later, more convenient time?

That's a perfect example of something that is not **straight talk**.

Straight talk is sourced by integrity which is actually a conversation for Chapter 4 - and which we will be going into in depth at that time. For now, what I will say about talking straight is this...

When you talk straight – you tell the truth, have empathy for others, and are complete in your communications. There is no cleaning up to do, no promises to break and clean up and, if there are, you make them in a timely manner, with respect and a commitment to keeping your word going forward.

Chapter 3 (Cont'd)

Ontologically speaking, this kind of communication is the source of power for you and your listener.

You may have noticed, in the world around you, that, while there are exceptions, what normally prevails around us is a world of a win/lose mentality.

That is because when human beings are in survival mode – **when our limbic brain kicks in** and tells us that others have to lose in order for us to win – that there is no win/win –**we lose sight of the possibility of contribution** and what giving to others and sharing our lives with others can provide.

As you become more and more aware of your thoughts - the ones that involuntarily come up - you will also become more and more aware of your ability to choose those thoughts you will act on and those you will ignore. This is truly when transformation becomes real.

Consider a quote by Elizabeth Bernstein in a New York Times article, *Doubt in your Head*, "If a huge truck pulled in front of you dangerously on the highway, you'd switch lanes quickly. You need to do this when negative thoughts arise."

She advises – as do I – that when you turn your mind immediately to something else, you defeat that kind of negative thought pattern.

Chapter 3 (Cont'd)

Think about a challenge you need to solve, plan a vacation, walk yourself through a fun project or a skill or hobby you love. Keep in mind **you cannot hold two thoughts simultaneously**. Replace those self-defeating thoughts with other, more empowering ones that YOU – not your subconscious – create.

From time to time, all of us stray into that dark place (**inside our heads, I mean**) and get stuck in negative thinking, paranoid delusions about what others think of us, and unhealthy critical reviews of our own actions, thoughts, appearances, etc. – you get the picture, right?

Well, keep in mind that, ontologically speaking, *YOU* **are not your thoughts**. You are HAVING those thoughts and they are NOT who you are.

Negative thoughts that undermine you, your effectiveness and your power, are merely memories, reactions and things from the past – designed to have you "survive."

Remember, that is ALWAYS the job of your limbic (reptilian) brain... to keep you alive! Any time IT perceives you are threatened in some way, physically, emotionally, or any other way, it will revert to what it knows from the past. No matter how debilitating those thoughts might be, the reptilian brain prefers those thoughts to anything "unknown."

Chapter 3 (Cont'd)

IT knows how to survive – because it did in the past, by making determinations from the past. IT does NOT want to consider that something in the future – some unknown – might be better, make you happier, or contribute in some way to your fulfillment. It cares ONLY for survival – at any cost.

Keep this in mind as you consider what we have learned about your "mind" and its commitment to keep you safe.

Gaining the ability to Communicate with Power
Ok, let's continue exploring the distinctions of powerful communications.

It could be said for human beings, **EVERYTHING depends on your level of communication, right?** Even when you are "in action," the actions you take are correlated to your conversations about who you are for yourself, and for others.

Let's look for example at the subject of integrity. Of course, integrity is a big subject and one we will be tackling in some depth in Chapter 4; but for now, suffice it to say that with regard to integrity, communication plays a major role.

For example, if you have an appointment and you can see you're going to miss it or be late.

Chapter 3 (Cont'd)

Communicating or letting someone know when you can be expected or that you are planning to be late, is important. It can mean the difference between someone respecting you or not – between someone making assumptions about you and how you treat your friends or colleagues.

Most of us know, for example, that if we are going to be late, we should call and let them know. The manner in which we do or don't do this can impact a career and a friendship and by communicating and letting someone know in plenty of time to avoid a major inconvenience, if possible, can end up being very important; yet most of us fail to take that into consideration.

Another important area of communication is being able to tell someone something that is "true" for you **without judging someone else** for his or her differing beliefs. **This is another key component in effective communication.** How many of us have disagreed with a friend and destroyed a friendship or a relationship in the process of communicating that; sometimes, even with no intention of wanting to do that but feeling helpless to prevent it?

These are small, real life examples of typical areas of communication where many of us fall down – and we are going to look at some of the tools that can support us as we begin to improve our communication skills.

Chapter 3 (Cont'd)

Managing results with speaking

Another area we want to talk about is "Speech Acts" – The following information will provide a powerful source for producing results. Speech acts are ways of speaking that "cause" things to happen as opposed to just "talking about" something. You are literally causing action by virtue of how you speak. Another way of saying this is to engage in "committed speaking;" that is, speaking in a way that generates a commitment to something occurring in reality, rather than just speaking in a random manner, with little or no intention to produce results [See end of Chapter 3 for more on "Speech Acts"].

An example of this kind of communication is "making a request." So, instead of saying, "Gee, we should have lunch sometime" (which produces literally nothing in the real world), if I say, "I'd like to have lunch with you on Tuesday at 11:00 AM – will that work for you?" actually produces a result.

Have you heard someone say, "I wish people would close the door when they come in" **and the door remains open with every person who enters?** Then the person who said that gets annoyed because no one is closing the door? That is because they don't even realize they never actually asked! That would be "Please close the door!" Simple, right? But something many of us never do.

Chapter 3 (Cont'd)

Another example is "making a promise" – A promise causes something to occur in the world, just by the nature of speaking it. When I make a promise, or give my word about something, the universe shifts to accommodate that promise – my listening of who you are shifts to accommodate it. Listen to the difference a promise makes to how you are "heard."

"I'll give you a call sometime next week." – As the listener, what do you hear? You hear no commitment, no real assurance that it will happen and an interpretation that you are not important enough to receive a confirmed lunch date. Now, what if I say, "I'll give you a call on Thursday before 5:00" – **As the listener, what do you hear?** You hear a promise and feel that it is much more likely to occur, AND it is likely you feel much more appreciated and acknowledged because of it. Just by making promises and requests you can make things happen – actually create certainty in the world – for both yourself AND for others. It is all in how you say what you say!

So, here's what there is to know about words that cause action: There are several of them; we have covered two so far and we are going to look at four of them here. You will find that, when you use them, you can alter how the world shows up for you and for others. The four we are covering are: **promises, requests, declines and/or counter-offers**.

Chapter 3 (Cont'd)

Declines and counter-offers are pretty self-explanatory and are powerful speech acts as well. They go along with "integrity" because they match up with "straight talk," right? We talked about this earlier. When you are asked to do something, and you decline, it has people be clear that you are being straight and setting up their expectations for what will or will not happen.

When you counter-offer, you are allowing for some new opportunity to occur that a decline does not, so it is always the preferable thing to do. That way if someone has asked you to do something you don't want or are unable to do, you can always counter-offer.

> **For example;**
>
>> I'd really like to help you move, and I will not be available to do that. However, once you have moved, I will be happy to help you put your things away. Will that help? Great – I'll be there on Thursday at 7 PM."

Can you see that this statement has integrity, provides support for your friend, AND makes something happen? That is the value of these speech acts. There are actually two more I want to cover and they are assertions and assessments.

Now let's look at the last two "distinctions" of communication I want to cover with you. These can – like the others – really alter the way you communicate and produce results in life. The two terms are **Assessments and Assertions.**

Chapter 3 (Cont'd)

First, let us look at an Assertion:

An assertion is a fact – something for which there is physical evidence of some sort. An assertion requires evidence. This is the "what happened" in an incident. The factual, real provable occurrences.

An assessment, on the other hand, is not a fact.

It is an assumption, belief, opinion or feeling about something.
It is a "story"or interpretation we tell about an occurrence or thing that happened.

Let's take a moment here to do an exercise on this distinction...

First, I want each of you to write down a story about something that happened to you that was upsetting and for which you got angry, hurt and/or upset. Use about four or five sentences to describe the incident. (I've given you the next whole page if you need it).

_____

_____

_____

_____

Chapter 3 (Cont'd)

Chapter 3 (Cont'd)

Chapter 3 (Cont'd)

Now put that aside for a moment – and let's address this professional business scenario together: **Let's suppose you are working for an organization and the following occurred...**

A meeting for Friday morning was set up on Tuesday by the Sr. Manager's Administrative Assistant and she says she sent out an email to everyone who was supposed to attend. You were out of the office on Tuesday and never got the email. When you got back on Thursday, you were really busy and unable to check your email for messages from when you were gone. The meeting was held on Friday morning and because you never got the message, you didn't attend.

You got into a lot of trouble and you looked bad to your boss because you did not go to the meeting because information was discussed that probably affected your department and you didn't have anyone there to represent you. He now thinks you are irresponsible and unreliable and, as a result, you ended up looking really bad when it wasn't your fault, and you think someone should have checked to make sure you got the message.

Now, I'd like you to ask yourself the following questions:
- What are the facts and what actually happened? **These are the assertions**.

Chapter 3 (Cont'd)

- What is the story about what happened? **These are the assessments.**

When you identify which is which, does that make a difference in the impact of the story? What do you see about that and how could it apply to your life?

[After you "highlight" what you think are the **"facts,"** check the answer on the last page of this Chapter.]

Can you see a way that this "story" could be rewritten to be more powerful in creating future success and results?

Now, let's look at the scenario you wrote about yourself and put aside. Go through that story and **highlight the assertions** (facts) and **the assessments** (opinions, thoughts, feelings etc.) What can you see differently about it now?   Write that down here.

_____

_____

_____

_____

_____

_____

Chapter 3 (Cont'd)

_____

_____

_____

_____

_____

_____

_____

_____

_____

As you can see, when you apply these two distinctions, there is just **what happened** and then what **we said about what happened**. Facts vs story. What could you say differently that would change the entire outcome or certainly change the way the situation occurred for you? Would that then give you more power under these circumstances?

Now, the next question that comes to mind is why you wouldn't have done that in the first place? Told exactly what happened rather than an assessment or story about what happened?

Remember, we talked about this before. **Because our mind gets in the way: Our mind wants to be right about how it isn't US who is responsible – it is someone else or something else.**

Chapter 3 (Cont'd)

That way we don't have to be the source for what we have. YET, THAT – **being the source for what we have or don't have** – is actually what gives us power in the world (How ironic is that, right?)!

So, we are now going to look at our lives today and how we can see that things are happening to us all the time – and, if we can see that even though things happen, we have the power to interpret them as we want or wish. **Taking responsibility for what is happening gives us power – blaming others does not.**

What do you see about this? Before we leave this powerful subject of communication, I am going to ask you to take another reading about where you think you are right now in level of responsibility.

Once again, we return to what we talked about in Empowerment Chapter 1 - **At what level of responsibility are you?**

Any movement that you've noticed? Are you resisting something? Are you "being right" about something? Not a problem - just notice it and jot down what you notice.

_____

_____

_____

_____

Chapter 3 (Cont'd)

Finally, there is one more "communication tool" that I have found over the years to provide a profound difference in the quality of my speaking.

It's called "Positive Re-framing."

Now, what do I mean about that? Let's consider the two-year-old, whose mother has spent the last 15 hours with their child indoors on a rainy afternoon. What do you think her most frequently used words have been? Most likely, if she is like me – or my mom – or her mom before her, the words are "NO!" Don't do that! or "No, you can't have that before dinner" or "No, no, no…don't touch that, you'll hurt yourself!" Well, you get the picture; I probably don't have to say more. As a matter of fact, a few years ago, a UCLA study verified that the average one-year old child hears the word "no" more than 400 times a day!   It's little wonder that by the time we hit school age, our negativity is firmly engrained in most of us.

So, while we do that to keep our children safe and to teach them what's important to avoid in life in order to be safe, when you consider all the negative messaging we give to our kids, you can begin to see how those "negative" mindsets get solidified over time - without our really meaning to have that happen.

Chapter 3 (Cont'd)

Let's look at the logic behind why that happens.

Sit back for a moment and I am going to give you some instructions that I want you to follow. Ready? Ok...

Do NOT picture a pink elephant.

Next, **do NOT see that pink elephant in a purple tutu**, dancing around in the middle of the jungle. Finally, I want you to NOT picture that pink elephant in a purple tutu NOT dancing around in the middle of the jungle with **a brown monkey, wearing a red hat,** jump on that elephant's back, **sticking a banana in that elephant's ear!**

Now, I'd be willing to bet that even though I told you NOT to picture that elephant and the monkey in the jungle, you would have been hard pressed NOT to have seen them, right? In some form or other. **Why do you think that is the case when you were instructed to not see them? Well, it's because the mind "thinks" in pictures.** When I ask you to think about eating a pizza – it's probable that you see a picture of a pizza – maybe your favorite kind – rather than picturing the words or letters P-i-z-z-a, right? It's that mind again. The one that – when you were little, allowed you to first understand language – in pictures – long before you could read or write. It is the fundamental language of the primitive brain. We all think in pictures.

Chapter 3 (Cont'd)

Now – and here's the best part of this conversation – the brain can only "see" the image of what you are talking about. **It cannot see a "NOT" image, right?** So, when I say, "Don't run in the street!" what does a child "see"? Literally, they "see" themselves or someone "running in the street!" That is definitely NOT the result you want, correct? No, you WANT them to do what? **STAY on the sidewalk!** Yet that is not what we usually say, is it? **"DON'T run down the driveway," Don't eat so fast" Don't leave your toys out."** We are constantly giving children instructions to picture what we want them to avoid – **RATHER than telling them what we WANT them to do.**

Can you see how much more powerful, persuasive and influential it can be to say what you DO want, rather than what you "don't?" This, then, is what is meant by **Positive Reframing**...AND, it works!

Let me tell you a quick story...

Shortly after I had taught this communication principle in a workshop several years ago, I received a call from a very grateful mother. She began by profusely thanking me for saving her child from what could have been a catastrophic fall. Evidently, the child – about 6 years old - had found his way out to the garage and climbed up on the roof of her SUV parked there.

Chapter 3 (Cont'd)

 Luckily, she saw him through a window in the kitchen door that led to the garage, and she ran after him. Breathlessly, she told me her first inclination was to yell – "Jonathan – DON'T JUMP!" as she saw him poised at the edge of the roof- and then she remembered this conversation and she stopped herself dead in her tracks.

She KNEW that if she said that, it is exactly what he would picture himself doing and she was clear about the outcome. She took a deep breath and, asked herself the question "What do I WANT him to do?" She then, said, **"Jonathan – SIT DOWN!"** – and he did…giving her time to run out to get him - preventing what could have been a very severe fall.

So, when I say that this way of speaking – saying what you do want – and the results you do want to create – DOES make a difference.

Consider some of our most famous linguistic instructional failures "Don't do Drugs" – "Don't Litter" – or how we often use phrases like "Don't Forget" or "Don't Jaywalk" or "Don't be selfish."

Perhaps more effective ways of saying these would be – "Stay Away from Drugs" "Put Litter in its Place" or "Remember to…," "Walk in the Crosswalk," or "Be generous."

Chapter 3 (Cont'd)

While it's true that changing a lifetime of "don'ts, can'ts, won'ts, shouldn'ts and wouldn'ts" takes some thinking and pausing and changing of habits. Like anything we have been talking about here, **the results you will reap as you practice growing your communication skills will be overwhelmingly rewarding...I promise!** They might even save you a trip to the emergency room with a 10-year-old with a broken arm *(Stay OFF the trees and play on the ground!).*

On the next page, I have included a worksheet so that you can practice Positive Reframing. **Write the corrections below the statements –** *and avoid peeking at the answers (I have included them at the end of the book)!*

Your attitude is like a box of crayons that color your world. Constantly color your picture grey, and your picture will always be bleak. Try adding some bright colors to the picture by including humor, and your picture begins to lighten up.

Allen Klein

Chapter 3 (Cont'd)

POSITIVE REFRAMING EXERCISE

1. I don't think we have enough milk for the week.

2. I won't be able to be there until after 7 AM.

3. I don't want you to misunderstand the point I'm making.

4. I can't hear you.

5. I can't wait more than 20 minutes for you.

6. I don't like that color dress on you.

7. Remember, you can't be late tonight.

8. Don't create confusion.

9. Don't forget to bring the book.

10. We shouldn't argue with our customers.

11. She's not doing her job.

12. It's not hard to do it correctly.

13. We shouldn't compete with each other.

Chapter 3 (Cont'd)

...and now, **on to your AffirmActions for Chapter 3**

Words are singularly the most powerful force available to humanity. We can choose to use this force constructively with words of encouragement, or destructively using words of despair. Words have energy and power with the ability to help, to heal, to hinder, to hurt, to harm, to humiliate and to humble.

Yehuda Berg

CHAPTER 3 - AFFIRMACTIONS & ASSIGNMENT

Chapter 3's AffirmAction is related to communication (of course)! It's time to begin communicating in a way that empowers yourself and others - Let's start with something you say that you frequently experience leaves some one person or others angry, upset or in reaction to you. Can you think of anything?

_____

_____

_____

_____

_____

_____

_____

_____

Ask yourself who you are being as you interact with that person. Are you being "right" about something and making someone else "wrong?" **Is there a better way?** Does it really matter who is right or wrong; is the relationship more important to you than being right?

Once you establish that the relationship matters, **you can begin to let go of old ways of being and clean up your unconscious ways of communicating with those you love**. Mostly those ways of being are based on past experiences and justifications - and leave you and others disempowered.

Chapter 3 (Cont'd)

AFFIRM: Determine how you want to be perceived and understood by those in your life whom you love. Creating relationships that work requires letting go of all anger, hurt, or righteousness and resentment. I think it was Ann Landers who said: "Hanging on to resentment is letting someone you despise live rent-free in your head." Anger and resentment fester and kill the joy in life.

> **Think about who you are for the people you love and create a statement that reflects that.** Write that statement down and repeat it to yourself at least 10 times. **For example:** *"I am someone who honors and loves others; regardless of whether I agree with their beliefs or not"* or *"Relationship is not about winning or losing, it is about love and support of the people in my life." Write whatever works for you and create it from your heart and not from being right about anything.*

ACTION: Make a list here of those people in your life with whom you have fractured relationships. It is time to clean them up. One by one, call or talk to them - in person - letting them know of your love for them and apologize for any way in which you have hurt them in the past.

_____

_____

_____

THE BOOK OF BEING...

Chapter 3 (Cont'd)

Chapter 3 (Cont'd)

Remember, you are taking responsibility for what you said that had them feel unwanted, unloved or unappreciated. **You do not have to agree with someone else's ideas, beliefs, or opinions - you can honor them exactly the way that they are without having to agree with them.** Letting them know you are sorry that you spoke in a way that had them feel less than is taking responsibility for how you spoke and does not lessen your value in any way. In fact, you are a bigger person for taking responsibility for how you said what you said.

**Footnote: As defined by John R. Searle in *Speech Acts: An Essay in the Philosophy and Language* (<u>John Searle</u>, Cambridge University Press, 1969)

Chapter 3 (Cont'd)

Answer Key to "What happened" vs "Story about what Happened" - **Assertions - based on facts (<u>underlined</u>)** /Assessments - opinions, feelings, guesses etc.(light)

[The Story] <u>A meeting for Friday morning was set up on Tuesday by the Sr. Manager's Administrative Assistant</u> and she says she sent out an email to everyone who was supposed to attend. **<u>You were out of the office on Tuesday</u>** and never got the email. When you got back on Thursday, you were really busy and unable to check your email for messages from when you were gone. **<u>The meeting was held on Friday morning</u>** and because you never got the message, **<u>you didn't attend.</u>**

You got into a lot of trouble and you looked bad to your boss because you did not go to the meeting because **<u>information was discussed</u>** that probably affected your department and **<u>you didn't have anyone there to represent you.</u>** He now thinks you are irresponsible and unreliable and, as a result, you ended up looking really bad when it wasn't your fault and you think someone should have checked to make sure you got the message.

Chapter 3 (Cont'd)

Actual Facts of What happened: A meeting for Friday morning was set up on Tuesday by the Sr. Manager's Administrative Assistant. You were out of the office on Tuesday. The meeting was held on Friday morning. You didn't attend. Information was discussed. You didn't have anyone there to represent you.

For the past 33 years, I have looked in the mirror every morning and asked myself: 'If today were the last day of my life, would I want to do what I am about to do today?' And whenever the answer has been 'No' for too many days in a row, I know I need to change something.

Steve Jobs

"Integrity is choosing courage over comfort; doing what is right over what is fun, fast, and easy; and adhering to the practice of honoring our word and our values rather than simply professing them."

Anonymous

EMPOWERMENT CHAPTER 4

The Journey to Integrity

[There is no "Destination" - There is only the Journey]

So, now that we've completed - for the time being - communications and how you can more effectively be responsible for what you say and how that impacts everything around you, let's take a look at that "mountain with no top!"

Now, what the heck do I mean by that? Kind of a strange visual, is it not - a mountain with no top? How exactly does that relate to this thing called Integrity and why should you care?

Well, strictly (and academically, speaking), a mountain with no top could be considered a "plateau" - at least according to Merriam Webster. And, as you well know, we don't put a great deal of store in what other people say things mean because, transformationally and ontologically speaking, *our* **working definitions** give us a great deal more insight and a place to create new possibilities; whereas the dictionary gives us "historical" decisions about what something has meant IN THE PAST… something we want to leave behind where it belongs!

Chapter 4 (Cont'd)

So, starting in this moment, let's take a look at what THEY say about the word "INTEGRITY."

Let's look at the **Dictionary definition of integrity:**

Integrity:
- ✓ The quality of adherence to strong and ethical principles; soundness of moral character; uprightness;
- ✓ **Synonyms:** honesty, rectitude, principles, ethics, morality, virtue,

Consider now, this: That integrity, very like "responsibility" as most of us have known and experienced it - from childhood - contextually - has, for most of us, been grounded in "ethics" or morality. Old Context: **It is good to have integrity. You are bad if you do not have integrity.** Pretty simple. Just be good, have integrity at all times, and your life will work out! *End of story!*

But is it?

What does it mean to have integrity? How does one determine how much integrity is enough and is it ever 100% complete?

Chapter 4 (Cont'd)

✓ If you keep your room and your house clean, does that mean you have integrity (even if you fudge on your income tax and say that lunch with your cousin Sally or Aunt Ethel was "business")?

✓ If you ALWAYS tell the truth, does that mean you have integrity (even if you don't brush your teeth and floss twice a day)?

✓ When you go to the grocery store and it is clear that a product is mismarked (too low) do you run to the butcher department and say, "Please charge me the right price for this piece of steak - it is priced too low"?

✓ Have you ever gone to the grocery store and gotten out to the parking lot with a package lodged in the bottom of your shopping cart that you know you did not pay for but which the cashier did not see, and you forgot to mention? Do you run right back in and say, "Can I please pay for this, you forgot to charge me for it?"

✓ When you pull into your garage, do you ever notice for the thousandth time what a mess it is and how you swore you would clean it up last weekend (and the weekend before, and the weekend before that)?

Ok, I'll stop.

Chapter 4 (Cont'd)

I know we all could probably think of a million ways all of us have a certain "lack of integrity" in our lives. How do I know that? We are human beings! No human being is perfect - well, hardly any - maybe your mom?

So, let's face it, when we look at 100% integrity - Our chances of getting to the top of the "integrity" mountain, is pretty much out of most poor mortals' reach. However, does that mean we should not strive to get there? To have integrity? **Does that mean it is a hopeless cause and why bother?**

Absolutely not. It is only when we focus on the **100%** AND **when we connect integrity to morality** that it is easy to lose hope. You can pretty much count on being stuck with judgments, "shoulds" and "should nots," and a whole lot of opportunities to criticize others; make ourselves - and, frequently, everyone else - bad and wrong when we see a level of **"integrity" that we think is "unacceptable" or what we say, is definitely imperfect or not good enough.**

And, if we consider, that, like responsibility, there is only the continual journey - the taking ground - without blame, fault, recrimination or reward - that **one can be powerful around a lofty goal, like integrity; the mountain with no top.** The mountain path upon which we all are traveling - some slipping back more than others - but all on the same journey together as human beings.

Chapter 4 (Cont'd)

Consider again this alternative or "created" definition for Integrity:

Integrity: The state of being whole, entire, or undiminished; like a circle, a sound, unimpaired, or perfect condition.

If we "try on" that *"working definition"* that integrity is "being whole and complete, with nothing left out," you could say then, that we are likely to be empowered to implement practices and take actions that support that wholeness and completeness.

When you remove blame or fault, and stop making someone wrong, something like freedom to increase our level of integrity can arise...

As it is with "Responsibility," when you remove blame, shame, guilt, or credit, etc. the DISTINCTION "integrity" - and restoring integrity - can then provide an opportunity for honoring something rather than making something – or someone - wrong.

Let me use a metaphor here that **Werner Erhard** used many years ago, which made perfect sense to me and maybe it will help you as well.

Chapter 4 (Cont'd)

He said (and I am paraphrasing here ...**Consider the bicycle wheel.** There are two primary parts; the "spokes" that lead from the center to the edge and the "rim."

Now, this wheel - **when it is "whole and complete" - all spokes aligned and true - will ride - a straight path.** If you remove or bend one or two of the spokes, the wheel will probably still "roll;" but the likelihood that its path will be "true" or "straight" has been diminished because it is no longer "whole and complete" with nothing left out. It may take you down the road a ways, but the ride will be a bit tougher, and the path will not be necessarily the one you meant to take because you may be pulled to one side or the other **trying to make up for the wheel that has lost its "integrity"- its wholeness.**

Think of your integrity - and your life - like that wheel.

The more integrous your life, the straighter you will travel in the direction you choose. The oftener you allow your integrity to "slip," and bend your values to accommodate convenience or circumstances, and the more you leave out or neglect those things you know are the things you would do if you followed your inner path, the more likely you are to encounter those bumps in the road, those twists and turns of misfortune and the mistrust of others.

Chapter 4 (Cont'd)

Remember, **it's a rare breed of human beings - almost non-existent as far as I can tell - for anyone to have 100% integrity at all times.** Merely being human beings, ontologically speaking, is reason enough to explain that, at times, we all fail the "integrity" challenge. We all slip back from time to time - After all, the "survival brain" sometimes causes chain reactions and disruptions to even the most determined souls among us.

You could consider it this way.

Once again, paraphrasing Werner - "Integrity is a mountain with no top - and we are all on the journey up or down."

Some of us are moving up or down a little faster than others and, make no mistake about it, we ARE all on it whether we are awake to it or not. **When our attention is on having integrity, it makes life a little bit easier for us and for others in our life.** When we are unaware that we are on the journey and unconscious that we are slipping back, things can get pretty tough.

Life just works when integrity is intact and while sometimes keeping it there can be a challenge, it's a game worth being awake for. **So, if Integrity is the mountain all of us are on, and we are always somewhere ON that mountain... either on the way up or on the way down...**

Chapter 4 (Cont'd)

it is helpful to know that neither way is better or worse; consider that life just works better when you are on the way up…

If we examine the word from the historical perspective - you know, how we usually think about it when we say someone is a "person of integrity;" **what comes to mind about that person?**

Well, for me, **I'd consider the personal characteristics; things like being truthful and honoring my word, authenticity, and doing what I say I am going to do** and if I don't, I expect to take responsibility for it and "clean it up," either by making a new agreement or apologizing and telling the truth about not intending to do what I said I would do. What about you? What behavior do you consider necessary to be considered a person of integrity?

Let's look at a list of what some of those areas might be for someone who demonstrates integrity…

People who have integrity...
1. Speak the truth
2. Behave honestly in

      ✓ Money transactions

      ✓ Exchanges of goods and services

      ✓ All manner of giving one's word

Chapter 4 (Cont'd)

3. Honor their promises

4. Honor agreements

✓ Acknowledge any changes/breaches and clean up any resulting messes

✓ Communicate to all concerned at the earliest possible time to let others know if they are not going to keep their word

5. Maintain a clean and orderly space – work and living

6.. Are complete in all relationships and refrain from leaving others upset or disempowered

7. Give their word authentically; ONLY say what they actually intend to do

8. Take actions consistent with their social conscience - and if they don't, would they clean it up

9. Speak only for themselves, avoid gossip, and are authentic

10. Make amends when they have unintentionally or intentionally injured someone else by word or deed

11. What would you add to this list?

_____

_____

_____

_____

_____

Chapter 4 (Cont'd)

_____
_____
_____
_____
_____
_____
_____
_____

What else would you say contributes to someone BEING a person of integrity while leaving OUT the morality and judgment of that?

_____
_____
_____
_____
_____
_____
_____
_____
_____
_____
_____

Chapter 4 (Cont'd)

Where would you say YOU are on the mountain and what do you think others would say OF you?

_____

_____

_____

_____

_____

_____

_____

_____

_____

_____

Are there areas to clean up and new promises to make, either to yourself or to others?

_____

_____

_____

_____

_____

_____

_____

_____

Chapter 4 (Cont'd)

What would it feel like to tell the truth about everything? Would it be a relief? Would it be frightening? Is there someone you could talk with about this so that you can clear it up and move "up" the mountain?

_____

_____

_____

_____

_____

_____

_____

_____

_____

_____

As long as we are talking about integrity, and asking the question...Is there anything you would like to clear up or tell the truth about?" (it's just too perfect an opening for me to pass up...) Who would you need to share this with to be "complete" and feel in total integrity?

_____

_____

_____

Chapter 4 (Cont'd)

Chapter 4 (Cont'd)

What is it an opening for? Why clearing the runway, of course!

> (So, now, I can hear you saying "Wow, we just finished talking
> about climbing a mountain with no top, now the crazy woman
> is talking about going to an airport and "cleaning a runway!")

Sorry, I was speaking metaphorically, only!

Here's what I mean.

If you WERE to go to the airport, you would see that there is
NOTHING on a runway to impede a plane from taking off, right?
AND, the reason for that is...? Because a plane needs a **clear
runway** to make it up into the sky - *just as YOU need a clear runway
to experience transformation in your life!* It's as simple as that! And
those things from your past that get in the way are those things you
need to "clean up" and get complete.

What do I mean by "get complete?" – I know, I've mentioned it before
That's because it is really important.

**Ok, let's go back to the dictionary and look at the word,
"complete" as distinguished from "finished" – A little review, so
to speak.**

Chapter 4 (Cont'd)

COMPLETE: Lacking nothing; **whole and perfect, exactly the way it is and exactly the way it is not;** nothing lacking, not requiring more work; entirely done. having all necessary parts, not lacking anything, unlimited, not requiring more work, entirely done or fully carried out

FINISHED: Having reached the end of an activity, job; concluded, **terminated, over with,** requiring no more work; doomed, condemned, brought to ruin (as in career or relationships) Hint: These last two are particularly useful!

Consider the following question...

How many relationships, jobs, projects and incidents from our past have we considered "finished" and yet, we know they are not "complete?" You do know what I mean, don't you?

We call them complete, don't we? **Actually, we pretend to ourselves they are complete -** and yet, sooner or later they come up again. They rear their ugly heads; whether it is a project or a relationship or a time we got fired, or a failure at work...

All of those "finished" incidents are still littering the runway of our lives; and getting in the way of us truly "taking off" into new possibilities.

Chapter 4 (Cont'd)

Well, this "distinction" is all about getting past those so called "finished" relationships, jobs, projects, etc., and getting truly complete. Making sure there is no garbage or junk in the way before you take off on your new life's journey.

So, as you ask yourself, "**What kind of garbage could be on the runway?**" Consider that anything that is **incomplete from the past, like** bills not paid, closets or rooms a mess, relationships ended in anger or resentment, or **anything at all that is incomplete,** will stop you as you get ready to take off.

That's why we are asking you to begin clearing up all areas of your life. This takes time and we invite you to get started NOW!

This includes incomplete projects, and un-communicated conversations with people in your life; including those who may no longer be in your life because they have died or because they are no longer in your life for other reasons.

In order for this to happen, you'll begin the process of "letting go" of past hurts, anger, grudges, and disagreements and begin cleaning up all areas in your life

On the following page are some ways this would show up in reality

Chapter 4 (Cont'd)

Begin this today…

- ✓ **Pay your debts or make promises to pay** those to whom you owe money

- ✓ **Clean your closets** and your room, house or apartment

- ✓ **Clean your car**

- ✓ **Communicate** with people in your life

  For example:
  - o Your parents and siblings
  - o Friends you have been meaning to be in communication with and haven't
  - o People you are avoiding
  - o People who you think are not worth being in communication with

When you start this process, many things could start to upset you.

If you have difficulty when you think about completing a conversation or letting go of something in the past, here is an exercise you can do to get it complete. This is a great opportunity to get complete with something or someone who came up when you asked yourself the question **"With whom or what am I incomplete?"**

Chapter 4 (Cont'd)

IMPORTANT NOTE: Regarding the success of this exercise: It will ONLY work if you are willing to get off any position you have about this issue and are willing to get complete.

Once you decide to take it on, you will be writing and saying everything related to this incident so make sure you set aside the time to do it completely. **You may believe that you have already said everything or done everything you know how to do** to get complete; however, if you had, this issue would still not be present in your experience as being incomplete. **Leave nothing unsaid - nothing undeclared - nothing unrevealed.**

Take all the time you need to say it all - even repeating those things you have said before and which still come up to say again.

GETTING COMPLETE

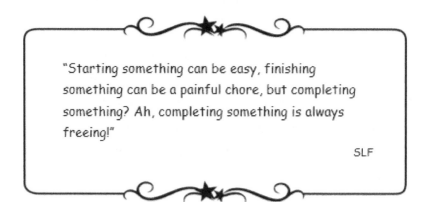

"Starting something can be easy, finishing something can be a painful chore, but completing something? Ah, completing something is always freeing!"

SLF

Chapter 4 (Cont'd)

Materials Needed for this Activity

- Pen
- Paper – I recommend you do not use your journal or the book for this assignment.
- Time: Usually a minimum of 60 to 90 minutes, depending on the issues at hand
- *Willingness* to move through - and let go of - emotions like anger, discomfort, upset, sadness & get "clear"

Take a moment now and think back to wherever you experience being incomplete about this issue or with this person.

It could be a previous relationship, a project that you never finished, a friend with whom you have unresolved anger or resentment, some issue you are angry about and have never addressed or have addressed yet it still occurs as "incomplete;" anything at all that comes up for you when you think about being finished with something and yet still "incomplete."

Turn to a clean page of a notebook. Trust me, that while I could give you some space to write here, it would probably be insufficient to get the job done and to get yourself complete!   This could be one of the most important things you get out of this entire book, so don't rip yourself off. Do it now... **Get ready to work.**

Chapter 4 (Cont'd)

Step 1:

At the top of the paper, write down – as close as you can remember – the date when the offending incident or "break" in relationship occurred or when you stopped working on what now occurs for you as "incomplete."

Step 2:

Think back to how you felt in that moment or at that time. Where were you? What were you feeling? Who was there and who was missing who you say should have been there? What, if any, decision did you make at that time – consciously or unconsciously- about what was happening or not happening? Who made that decision?

Now, write down everything you were feeling at that moment. Everything. Your feelings, your decisions, assessments, assertions, your interpretations.

What you think it meant that this happened or didn't happen, who did it happen to and who else was involved? **Write down everything you remember about the circumstances and how you felt about them.** Write until you have said everything there is to say. Write it all down, as if no one will be judging or seeing it. Just say what you think and most importantly how you feel about whatever it was and how you felt then and feel now about it.

Chapter 4 (Cont'd)

Get it ALL written. If there is anything left, write that as well. It doesn't matter if it is repetitious, badly or well written, true or not true; this is you writing about how you felt or feel now and what you realized or felt was true at the moment. Get it all written down. Don't stop until you have said everything you either already said, never said before, or wanted to say – or said, but didn't feel got heard.

Step 3:

Read back every word of what you said. Read it out loud to yourself. Listen to what you said. After you have read the entire document, notice if there is anything left unsaid or if there is anything left out. If so, write it down. Read what you added and see if it is now all said.

Step 4:

Reflect on everything you said.

Was that the first time you have ever experienced feeling that way about something? Is that the first time you or someone else close to you has ever made a decision like that? Can you remember an earlier similar experience? Sometime when something happened like this or you made a choice like this before?
If yes, do the following...

Chapter 4 (Cont'd)

What was that earlier experience? Describe it now – in the same detail and with the same complete description of your feelings etc. at that time. Go through Steps 1 through 4 again with the earlier incident as well.

If no, notice if you are still upset and/or incomplete with the current incident or incompletion. If you are still incomplete or upset, read the entire thing again. Continue adding to your document until you are clear and no longer upset. **You WILL get there, and some issues take longer than others.**

Consider that if you said "yes," something from the past is likely to be coloring your present. That you may not be upset merely about what you thought you were upset about. It could be that something else, which occurred much earlier, is lurking behind the scenes, in your subconscious mind, and continuing to dominate your current behavior or feelings.

Consider that if you said "no," and you are not complete, there is something you have not yet said about the incident or incompletion. Continue writing about it, making sure that you express everything and say all that there is for you to say about it, without judging or evaluating what you have written.

Keep going... you can do it.

Chapter 4 (Cont'd)

Step 5:

Once you no longer experience the strong emotions connected with this incident or person or feel that you can "let go" of the anger, upset or emotions around this issue, you are "clear" and you can move forward.

If you are so inclined, and you see that there is an opening to communicate to someone about something, do that. **Keep in mind that often we are upset about something or with someone who knows nothing about it** so there may be an opportunity to communicate with them. However, most of the time when we are incomplete with something or someone, they know about it and getting complete with them – in partnership – can be an amazing experience for everyone.

<u>A word of caution</u> - Consider our earlier conversation about the levels of responsibility – **Empowerment Chapter 1**. If you are going to speak to someone about this incompletion, **make certain you are at Level 2 of responsibility when you have that conversation.**

Are you clear about why this is important? Can you see an area that might be a problem? Take the time to do this assignment; as I said, it could be one of the most important you do in this program!

Chapter 4 (Cont'd)

What do you see or notice about this exercise? Write it here and **acknowledge yourself** for getting off your position and allowing yourself to get complete! Congratulations!!

_____

_____

_____

_____

_____

_____

_____

_____

_____

_____

_____

_____

_____

_____

_____

_____

_____

_____

_____

_____

Chapter 4 (Cont'd)

_____

_____

_____

_____

_____

_____

_____

_____

_____

And now… another step in your journey… **_Gratitude!_**

Exercise 2: It is time to develop a deeper appreciation for all that you have in your life. Begin each night to write a list of those things for which you are grateful.

We will be developing this conversation more deeply as we explore the Law of Attraction further on in the program. For now, though, begin listing those things each day that you experience gratitude for having in your life.

List a minimum of 3 to 5 things each day and do not repeat any one of them for at least a week.

Chapter 4 (Cont'd)

Plan on setting aside time each day before bed to record these things for which you are grateful.

_____
_____
_____
_____
_____
_____
_____
_____
_____
_____
_____
_____
_____
_____
_____
_____
_____
_____
_____

Congratulations - We're getting close to moving on to Empowerment Chapter 5!

CHAPTER 4 – AFFIRMACTIONS & ASSIGNMENT

This Chapter was all about getting complete with the past and making room for new relationships and a new level of integrity in your life.

AFFIRM: Before going to sleep, notice where today you were honest and truthful with someone even though it was difficult and acknowledge yourself for being authentic and having integrity. Notice as well if there was someplace that you failed to be honest and truthful; where integrity was missing.

> Did you gossip? Talk about someone else, leaving something behind in someone else's space about a third party who was not present? Gossip ruins lives and impacts relationships.

Saying anything about anyone without their permission or them being present is gossip. Resolve with yourself to avoid doing this ever again. Affirm that by creating a statement that you can repeat to yourself when faced with that choice in the future. Here is an example: **I am someone who honors my word and my relationships, and I clean it up when I fail to do so** or **I am someone who always avoids gossip or talking about someone behind their back.** I honor people and who they are in the world and do nothing to diminish them either within or without their presence.

Chapter 4 (Cont'd)

ACTION: Take one action every day that increases your level of integrity. Notice where you step over the line and pull back. Make a list of those areas in your life where you can see that you are out of integrity. Where you have not done what you said you would or where you have made promises you did not keep either to yourself or to others. Keeping your word with yourself is where integrity begins. Clean it up and begin a practice of putting integrity in place in areas where it has been missing.

> **If you have gossiped about someone, take the time to tell them.** Clean it up; apologize and give your word that you will not do so again. Go to the person to whom you gossiped and apologize to them for leaving them with something about someone else that would otherwise not have been there.
>
> Begin noticing in your life where you are not responsible for what you say about others and begin a new practice of integrity.

Be sure to check out the Integrity Worksheet I have included at the end of the book – and USE it!

EMPOWERMENT CHAPTER 5

Why Dwell in the Past When There is only NOW?

[Distinguishing Past Present Future]

One morning I woke up with a pounding heart, thinking I was missing something...some undefinable thing that I forgot to do, or buy or something I left behind somewhere.

What it was, I have no idea - I only know something was amiss - and it felt... odd and dislocating.

Experts sometimes say that the "déjà vu" **experience** is merely crossed wires or brain patterns that have gotten mixed up and maybe that's what it was... mixed up brain waves. All I know is, as illogical as it seemed at that moment, I tried to go back to sleep; thinking that something would "click" and I would be able to re-capture whatever it was that I had forgotten or that had just slipped away as I awoke from whatever dream I was having at the time.

Of course, it was pretty darn useless. **Whatever it was had gone; never to return.** Not even the memory of the dream remained.

Chapter 5 (Cont'd)

I then noticed I started to make something up - hoping that it would trigger something - nothing useful came out of that, of course, and I finally gave up.

How often do we attempt to "go back" - wish we could relive a moment or change a decision or react differently to something that produced a life altering result?

For many of us, it's a common occurrence - and mostly, we're unconscious that we do that. **Have you ever locked your keys in your car and then grabbed quickly for the handle to open it - even though your conscious mind knows that the door has already locked after you?**

I remember standing in the cold late afternoon air one day while I was trying to get all the packages out of my car, fumbling with my wallet, and dropping things left and right - while my infant son was sitting patiently in his little car seat - waiting for me to come around to his side of the car and pick him up and out... **Then, finally, I had everything in my hands and slam, click... I shut the door and within a millisecond I realized what I had done.** The car keys? Sitting on my seat where I had laid them to pick up my packages - now, unreachable and in the closed Volkswagen Beetle, sealed tight as a bug in a rug... along with my 6-month-old baby boy! AND, what was the first thing I did?

Chapter 5 (Cont'd)

I grabbed the door handle and pulled - hoping against hope that I could go back that one second before and open the door. I KNEW it was locked, of course. I had heard it happen, had realized immediately what I had done - but my "mind" still had the thought that I could get in if I just reacted fast enough - **if I just could go back a half a second in time...**

Needless to say, I managed to get my keys and my baby out with a little maneuvering - however, that is not the point of this story.

The point is - that the mind does not recognize "past" as something that does not exist in the present. The mind imbues "past" with a non-existent reality and allows us to experience that "thinking" about the past, telling stories about the past and remembering the past is ALMOST the same as actually returning to the past. As if the past was still there - waiting for us to walk back into it... AND, we all know - logically - that is not true. However, if you think about it, on a daily basis we think about it, dwell on it, spend hours "if only-ing," remembering, and wishing to one degree or another, that we actually could change the past in some way if we think about it long enough, envision it sharply enough or wish it strongly enough.

Yet, logically, we do know that is not true.

Chapter 5 (Cont'd)

The past does not exist anywhere in time... It only exists in one place... In our language - our conversations about it. Conversations we have with ourselves and others. In that way, we keep the past "alive" - and we keep ourselves trapped in a never ending vicious circle of "what-ifs" and "if-onlys."

Check out these photos...

Consider as you look at them..., Where do you think those individuals were?

Were they thinking about the past?
 Were they wishing they were
somewhere else? Worrying about the time? Or what they will be doing in an hour?

Chapter 5 (Cont'd)

No, they are - no kidding - IN the present, "on the field" of rooting for their team and **being alive in this moment.**

The only real "time" we actually have.

Keep in mind, we are talking about **"being on the field"** as being truly IN their life at the moment; not contemplating their life, not thinking about what to do with their life, but truly BEING in it, in this very moment.

I would like you to take the case, that there is NO past. There is only now - this moment - and the life we create moment to moment in the successive moments of now we DO have.

So, is there a future? Waiting for us to walk into it? Not any more than there is a past waiting in the wings for us to walk back into it or change it. No future and no past - and yet, our lives are dominated by what we have or have not accomplished in the past, and what we want to have in our future.

AND, all the while, we are missing the one most precious time of all - the PRESENT!

So, let's take a moment here to more clearly define this conversation as 'past, present & future' as a distinction.

Chapter 5 (Cont'd)

According to Merriam, here is what we would read...

DICTIONARY DEFINITION: Past, present, future - A described span of time...

Past: Having existed or taken place in a time before the present

Present: Existing or happening now

Future: A time that is to come; the period of time that comes after the present...

And, if we were to create a "working definition" for what we mean by past, present, future, here is what that would distinguish for us:

WORKING DEFINITION: Past, present, future:

> **Past:** A memory, description or interpretation of a memory about a person, place or thing that no longer exists
>
> **Present:** Successive moments of now
>
> **Future:** An agreement - in language - of hope that another moment after this one will exist

In order to distinguish being present and being in the here and now, we require **conscious awareness** of the ontological tendency for human beings to conduct their lives as if the past and future are as real as the present, when, in fact, they do not exist on in reality at all.

Chapter 5 (Cont'd)

Stop and think about that for a moment. My guess is that your first instinct (limbic brain kicking in with full force, by the way), when you hear that statement is "That's CRAZY! Of course, the future exists or will exist - and certainly the past DID exist."

Consider this and try it on like a new concept.

Try it on that the past and future are merely a function of language; a mental or verbal construct; conversations we have with ourselves and others. For example, for a dog, there is no future. There is only right now. A bone, right now. A cat to chase, right now. Food to eat, right now. All that is real is the present; successive moments of now and being 'present' to that distinction requires language and conscious awareness. Until, of course, like us, **they dream and their unconscious brain replays memories and tapes from the past;** literally conversations we have with ourselves about what has occurred in times gone by with no reality in the present moment.

Can you see why it would be important to know this? Why and how it could make a difference for us to live with an **awareness of this in real time** and to continually pull ourselves back to the reality that the past is a conversation and **not something that is not currently in existence somewhere**, waiting for us to examine it further, define what something may have meant and who we may have been when something   happened to us in the past?

Chapter 5 (Cont'd)

What if we consider that all these are interpretations, beliefs, and assumptions made in the present moment; stories we make up that allow the "past" to make sense in our personal construct of "the way things are" and the way "we are" and the way the people in our lives "really are."

Whew! Quite a concept to grasp, isn't it?

Right now, for most of us, our limbic brain could be going crazy - dealing with the uncertainty that this conversation causes; the fear that there is something so alien - so strange as the statement that there is no past. That there is just our story or interpretation about what happened "back then"?

So, if we take the case that it IS "true" - which we are not saying. We are asking you try this on, like an experiment. What if there was no past - where would you be limited?

Of what would you be capable? Well, if you can't look to the past to determine what you are capable of, where would you look?

How would you determine if there was something you could or could not do? You would do what? Try it, right? You would make the attempt - at anything - anything at all that caught your interest, right? Think about it.

Chapter 5 (Cont'd)

Consider young children - seeing the possibility that they can walk.

For them, without language yet, there is no past. They have no stories about what they are capable of or able or unable to do. There is only the desire to get up and move to another place - to stand on their feet as they see others do and move. So, they pick themselves up and they fall. Then, they pick themselves up and fall again. What do you think they have that mean about themselves?

NOTHING!

They pick themselves up, dust themselves off and start all over again - until they walk! No past, no future, just walking! Imagine the possibilities if we continued to live our possibilities that way!

In a side note about being "present" - In *"The Power of Now,"* a book by Eckhart Tolle, he describes the state of presence, and our ability to understand that we are not our "mind" - I highly recommend this book as a way to expand this journey we are taking together toward transformation. It is an excellent tool and one that will continue to expand what we are talking about here in being present in this moment. And the reason I bring him up at this time is that I want to talk to you for a moment about gratitude, generosity and contribution from others.

Chapter 5 (Cont'd)

So, for example, when we experience being grateful, consider that when you have that experience - having gratitude - for something, you are present; literally present, to what is occurring right now. That is, completely conscious in the present moment. That is where gratitude exists. Even if you are grateful for what you have had in the past, *WHEN* you are being grateful or being conscious of being grateful, is right now. So why am I bringing that up?

Well, regardless of what we are grateful for, it, and everything else, is present in this moment and NOW is the only moment we really ever have.

To take it to the next level - from having gratitude in the moment and in coming from a way of being grateful - those are two different things, right? **One is momentary and fleeting - and one is a part of who you are constituting yourself to be - a "being"** who is, moment to moment, living in gratitude for everything in your life; literally **generating a way of "being" in life**.

So, if we look at "being" or coming from being someone who is a grateful human being and saying, "thank you" for something, which is showing gratitude as a momentary experience, we can see that these two things are quite different.

Being vs Doing - 2nd level

Chapter 5 (Cont'd)

Using gratitude as the instrument, I'd like to take a few minutes to expand on what we spoke of earlier as the difference between being and doing. This powerful distinction can be a challenge to verbalize – but I am going to attempt it now.

When you express having gratitude, in the moment, you are actually thinking about it. You may have received a gift, or you may have gotten something you wanted or something you desired may have occurred. A job perhaps, a girl or boyfriend gave you their number – some one thing that you are grateful for. **That is something you are doing**. It could be said that you are taking an action of sorts – or verbalizing, to yourself or others that you are grateful for something.

Being, on the other hand, is a state of mind. It is a place to come from within yourself – and it is an internal state that does not shift with whether you did or did not get something you wanted.

Gratitude as a state of being is something you experience being present always – even in your dark times. When you come from a place of gratitude – when who you are BEING is grateful, then even when times are difficult, you are grateful for having the opportunity to experience and overcome whatever the circumstances with which you are dealing.

Chapter 5 (Cont'd)

Can you now describe to me the difference between being and doing?

In its simplest terms, being is a state of mind and doing is an action you take.

Now, you might ask "why does it matter?" Whether you are being grateful for example or just "doing" or showing gratitude? Well, since we are energetic beings – as we have talked about earlier, you vibrate at a certain level. This stands to reason, right? Just as my mood impacts the level of my vibration and yours, it impacts how that vibration impacts my life and the lives of those around me.

When you come from a way of being that is grateful, your vibration is quite different than when you come from dissatisfaction and unhappiness.

Can you see that?

So, the more you can be aware of your way of "being" the more powerful you will be in directing your life and its outcome.

Let's look into this conversation a bit further – about how your way of being affects your life and the lives of others.

Chapter 5 (Cont'd)

Being as a State of Mind

If we return for a moment to something we have discussed earlier – being responsible - one of the ways we can be responsible is to look at how we occur for others or "show up" in life. In other words, **being responsible for our state of mind.**

For example; Have you ever known someone who appears to be angry most of the time?

You could say that someone who is angry sees the world in such a way that, for them, anger is appropriate. **If you ask them, they are likely to say they are not angry.** If you follow them around, though, you will notice that they find situations to be angry about and for which they take no responsibility. **You could say that they attract such circumstances to themselves.**

Here's another example: Have you ever known someone who consistently shows up as a "victim" of something? If anyone gets the flu, it is them. If anyone gets robbed, it is them. If anyone gets lost, it is them. **Does that sound familiar?** It could be said that they are a "victim" waiting to happen and they refuse to see that they have attracted that. Much like the person who is "anger" waiting to happen, this person carries with them what we could call a "way of being" that has them show up that way in the world.

Chapter 5 (Cont'd)

Consider it this way; the energy you give out determines the results you get. Consequently, we could say that someone who considers himself a victim in life, not responsible for what happens to them, will continue to attract being a victim.

So, if you look at your life, and especially what you have that you don't want in your life, from the point of view that you are "responsible" for all of it, what do you see?

Is there something you have been unwilling or unable to be responsible for in your life?

It's really important here - as we talk about being responsible for everything in our lives - to understand that when we speak about being responsible, it is not about being at fault. We introduced this in Chapter 1, remember?

Mostly, we are unaware that we are not coming from a way of being in that we are responsible for what we have in our lives. Many times, we keep on doing what we have always done because it is familiar. Mostly the past is comfortable because even when it brings unwelcome things, we know how to deal with them. Mostly, change is uncomfortable. We prefer to stick with what is familiar. As the saying goes, the "devil that we know is better than the devil that we don't know."

Chapter 5 (Cont'd)

You might even see that sometimes what we don't want continues to be what shows up because that is what we are attracting by who we are being, what we are doing, feeling, and saying, **often without realizing it.**

An example of this condition could be found in the statistics about family abuse. Frequently, statistics show that people who have had abuse problems in the past often gravitate toward people who have abusive tendencies, even years after the originating incident. Being "familiar" - almost comfortable - with that experience, they know how to deal with it – AND they are unsure how they could cope with another, unknown, experience. **So, they keep attracting it.**

A lot has been written over the past several years on **the Law of Attraction (LOA) - and if you've read any of it, you may know exactly what I am referring to.** If so, remember our conversation about bringing your "beginner's mind" to our program? Consider this is the first time you have heard about it and perhaps you will get something at a deeper level than ever before - or not. I'd say it depends on your intentions.

Let's look here at some of the information available on the subject, shall we?

The Law of Attraction – LOA - is said, by some, to have its basis in a quantum physics theory "like   attracts like."

Chapter 5 (Cont'd)

They maintain it has been proven by the "double slit" experiment, in which an "energy" wave (laser beam) is directed at a metal screen with two slits. This "barrier" causes the beam to split into two separate "energy waves" as they pass through the slits and then, once they pass through the barrier, come back together on the other side; combined into a single wave - (like attracts like).

I mention this only by way of explanation of what some "believers" have said; I am by no means an expert in the field of quantum physics. **I do know, however, that my experience with those who live their lives as if the LOA is "true" for them, have the experience of having power over the circumstances that surround them on a daily basis.** So, whether it is the "truth" that "like attracts like;" that the energy you put out will attract like energy back to you, could be, as I said earlier, like gravity. Unseen, and experienced many times over in life by me and many others.

If you consider it as a tool to guide you as you move forward - keeping your energy positive - you may find that, as others have before you, the Law of Attraction is one more tool in your toolbox for attracting the life that you want.

Consider as well, from this same perspective, that if **who you are being in life is grateful,** then you will continue to attract those

Chapter 5 (Cont'd)

things in life that you are grateful for - even those things that, initially, you have difficulty in seeing as having value of any sort.

There may be something hidden from your view that, with passing time, may reveal itself as a gift you are unable, at first, to see.

Consider the story of Amy Purdy, World Champion snowboarder, who at 19 years of age contracted Neisseria meningitis, a disease that affected her circulatory system and caused her to lose her both kidneys and her spleen and who had to have both of her legs amputated below the knee. Doctors had given her a 2% chance of survival, yet, two years later, after receiving a kidney transplant from her father and prosthetic legs, she finished third in a snowboarding competition at Mammoth Mountain. Despite losing her legs, she is a world champion adaptive snowboarder; healthy and grateful to be living the life of her dreams!

As we complete the conversation on the Law of Attraction, gifts and gratitude, we're going to explore one more "G" word... Generosity. We'll look at that in Empowerment Chapter 6.

For now, let's get started on our AffirmActions for Chapter 5 and your Assignment.

Chapter 5 (Cont'd)

It's factual to say I am a bilateral below the knee amputee. I think it's subjective opinion as to whether or not I am disabled because of that. That's just me.

Aimee Mullins (Athlete & Model)

CHAPTER 5 - AFFIRMACTIONS & ASSIGNMENT

This Chapter was all about being present, having gratitude for all that you have and being generous to others.

Being present means letting go of the past and being alive and awake to the present moment; living in a world exactly as it is "happening" in this very moment. How can you be awake to that each moment of every day? You create it as a habit and it begins with this affirmation. Before going to sleep, notice if you are thinking about what you failed to do for the day - notice if you are worrying about tomorrow. At waking up, notice whether you are thinking about all the things you have to accomplish for the day ahead or whether you are worrying about doing it all. Remind yourself by this affirmation that there is no past and whatever did not get done today does not exist; it is in the past and has no bearing on the present reality. What you are going to do later today is not what you are doing in this moment. In this moment, you are being present.

AFFIRM: Affirm this by creating a statement that you can repeat to yourself when faced with thinking about the past and/or fretting about the future. Here is an example of an affirming statement: **"I live in the present; the past and future are unreal. Only the present exists for me...it is a gift to be alive - and in the here and now."**

Chapter 5 (Cont'd)

Create an affirming statement now...

_____

_____

_____

_____

_____

_____

_____

_____

_____

_____

_____

ACTION: Get complete at the end of the day.

At bedtime: Take a moment before you sleep to acknowledge what you did get done, what you accomplished and completed. Take time to remember what you said you wanted to do and did not do. Then consciously agree to "let it go." **If you find you cannot let it go, write it down on a piece of paper and resolve that tomorrow you will schedule it to be done. Then let it go.**

Next. either sit or lay in your bed, feeling the sheets under you.

Chapter 5 (Cont'd)

If you are sitting, feel the floor under your feet. Notice it. **Then bring your awareness to your breath**. Breathe in for 4 counts and out for 6. This removes the stale air from your lungs and brings in new, fresh, oxygen into your blood. Do this for 3 to 5 minutes. Notice the air around you and how it feels to be alive in this moment. The only moment there is! **Appreciate your aliveness and your body. Then let go and relax.**

At arising in the morning: Find a sunny spot if you can and sit near it either in the house or outside. Put your feet on the floor or ground and take a deep breathe. **Get present to the morning - and the new day.** You are alive and ready to take on what's next.

Breathe in for the count of 4 and out for 6... Notice the sounds around you - listen for life. If you have access to music, play something classical for 5 minutes and just listen to the music.

Be present; appreciate your life and the opportunities that await you in the new day. **Experience and celebrate being alive in this** moment and remember that it is all that we really have.

Now, read the following quote and give some thought to all that we have said about being present in this moment...

Chapter 5 (Cont'd)

"I think midlife is when the universe gently places her hands upon your shoulders, pulls you close, and whispers in your ear:

I'm not screwing around. *It's time. All of this pretending and performing – these coping mechanisms that you've developed to protect yourself from feeling inadequate and getting hurt – has to go.*

Your armor is preventing you from growing into your gifts. I understand that you needed these protections when you were small. I understand that you believed your armor could help you secure all of the things you needed to feel worthy of love and belonging, **but you're still searching** *and you're more lost than ever.*

Time is growing short. There are unexplored adventures ahead of you. You can't live the rest of your life worried about what other people think. You were born worthy of love and belonging.

Courage and daring are coursing through you. You were made to live and love with your whole heart. It's time to show up and be seen."

Brené Brown, author

Next, go to your computer or handwrite the following words –

"I will open my heart and mind to new experiences … THIS IS IT!! Right now, this moment…is all I have!!!

Post this somewhere you can see it every day for as long as you are reading this book! See the Gratitude quotes at the end of the book.

EMPOWERMENT CHAPTER 6

Generosity – A Two Way Street

Years ago - and for many of them - I worked in corporate offices. I spent a lot of my time writing, designing and delivering training for managers, corporate executives and supervisors; teaching communication, coaching and developing curriculum that would enable them to be better leaders and make a difference with their staff. I spent many late hours working, long after most others in the company had gone home. As you can imagine, I'd been called a "workaholic" by some, overly diligent and a "brown-noser" (disgusting term, by the way) by others; basically, I worked 60 to 80 hours a week with little or no let-up - and frequently even spent time at the office on weekends as well, catching up with "odds and ends" I hadn't finished during the week.

During the day, whenever one of my employees or fellow staff members asked me for time off for something, I noticed I really was resentful. Frequently, I'd find myself thinking "I work really hard every day - I don't take extra lunch hours or extra time off - why should they?" Sometimes I'd feel a little guilty for feeling that way because I know it sounded selfish - but, still, that was how I felt.

Chapter 6 (Cont'd)

Sometimes, after I'd turned down someone's request for a favor or for some time off, I might think "Hmm, maybe I could have been more thoughtful or more flexible; maybe I should have given them what they asked for." - but, of course, by then, it was too late and the opportunity had passed.

One night, sitting alone in my office, after a particularly unpleasant day - when my assistant had asked me for an extra half hour for lunch, which I grudgingly (and ungraciously) gave but hated doing it, I wondered, "Why do I feel this way?" What could I do about this feeling - this resentment that I just couldn't seem to shake whenever someone asked me for a favor or time off or something that was not really within the bounds of what I was obligated to give.

I wondered, "Am I really a grouch? I know I am justified - I'm definitely "right" about how they shouldn't be asking for favors all the time. After all, I don't! Then why do I feel so guilty - and why don't they understand that I am right about this? I'd like to feel differently - but I just can't seem to change or shake that resentful feeling."

I decided to stop what I was doing - put my work aside and really notice my thinking about it. I was definitely being "right." That alone should have been a hint that something was "off" since I do know that when I am being "right" I am definitely making someone else "wrong" and that seldom works for anyone!

Chapter 6 (Cont'd)

So, I decided to coach myself.

I asked "What would I do if one of the people I was coaching told me that this heavy resentment was how they were feeling? What would I ask them and how would I coach them to feel differently? I decided I would ask myself "what was missing, the presence of which would make a difference?"

The answer came to me immediately - **What was missing was generosity.**

Here's what I noticed.

If we consider - as a distinction - the word **"generosity"** - there are actually two different perspectives or points of view. **One is what we give to others** and the **second is what we give to ourselves**.

Mostly we consider the first perspective as the authentic way to determine if one is "generous" - what do we give and how often - to others. We almost never look at the 2nd perspective - what do we give to ourselves? Yet, the 2nd perspective - what we give ourselves - might be a good place to look if I find myself "lacking" in generosity toward others!

Here's how the mechanism works.

Chapter 6 (Cont'd)

Take the case that I am "stingy" with myself. I don't allow myself to relax during the day - I drive myself constantly, to produce more, to make more money, to always be "delivering the goods." In other words, I rarely give myself a break! Then, when others ask for something or want something, it's really easy to be "righteous" and justified that I work hard, I don't take time off, I always have my "nose to the grindstone," so why shouldn't they?"

Wow! Pretty obvious. I began to see how that could lead to me resenting or begrudging others for what they want or what they would like to do? Then, I started playing with the idea that if I took off an hour during the day to run an errand, and I allowed myself the freedom to leave early or take the weekend completely off, **how would that impact my willingness to allow others to do the same?**

I began to get clear that if I did begin to show some generosity of spirit for myself, I just might be much more likely to feel generous toward them. I will have had the experience of what that is like, I will have allowed myself that freedom - and have been "generous" with myself.

What a concept, right? You would think I would have thought of that before! But here's the thing; I had been so busy "doing my thing" and acting automatically, I had not even realized how I was sabotaging myself.

Chapter 6 (Cont'd)

So, I could see that the next step was to give my theory a try. The next day, after having this internal conversation with myself, I took off an hour for lunch. No grabbing a sandwich and eating at my desk. I actually went out, sat in the park and enjoyed my lunch! I had all kinds of thoughts that everyone in the office would be really upset and think I had some nerve doing that when I barely EVER let them take the time to do that.

Here then is the amazing thing. When my colleagues noticed, they were happy - they generously acknowledged me - and said how great it was to see me out from behind my desk and enjoying the day! Wow, what an awakening. THEY knew the whole time and it was me who was blind to my automatic way of "being." I was able to see that by being generous to myself, I allowed that same possibility to occur for others.

By being stingy with myself, I literally had seen the same "way of being" reflected back to others.

Needless to say, it became clear to me that I now had a new piece of training for my up and coming managers, my executives and my trainees - and I was the perfect example of what is possible when "transformation" happens for a human being!

Chapter 6 (Cont'd)

Once again, as always, when we are awake to our own automatic behavior, we get the chance to choose and to impact others with the change we make in ourselves!

and now...

INTO THE GAP!

Well, you've made it a little more than halfway through your program - Congratulations! I really invite you to acknowledge your progress and to notice where your actions or ways of "being" have shifted since you began.

- Are you more conscious?
- More present?
- Do you notice when you are not being in the moment and when you are contemplating the past?
- Have you begun "clearing the runway" or are you still dragging the past with you when you get up every morning and see all the things that you said you would complete... all the relationships you said you would "clean up," all the actions you said you would take and have not?

So, what exactly is this "gap" I keep referring to?

Chapter 6 (Cont'd)

There are actually a few ways to look at it. Let's begin there, ok?

Consider that "the gap" *could* be **the place between the present** (*being conscious about what is actually "so" in your life right at this very moment)* - or **the condition in which you are currently existing** - AND the **future you are in the midst of creati**ng - (*out of an intention or a commitment)* - that exists - at this very moment - **only in language or what you say about it.**

So, another way of saying it is: The future you are creating in your speaking does not yet exist; It is just an idea - a possible outcome of actions you have yet to take, based on what you say or have declared that you want as a future.

Between what is so, right now - and what you want, in the future - is the "gap" you are standing in! It is actually pretty simple. You could say that the **"gap"** represents a life before you take action to achieve what you are committed to and that "gap" is also a language phenomenon. There is not really a "gap" or a physical space you are standing in or on; it is a language phenomenon that, when you acknowledge you are there, can empower you to move forward in creating what's next for your future based on what you say you want rather than a default mode or what circumstances or the past dictates you can have.

Chapter 6 (Cont'd)

Take a few minutes here to create that "gap" for yourself.

Let's get grounded in what's real - in this very moment.

Read the next 3 sentences out loud. When you finish them, take a deep breath and be quiet for a minute. Then take step 2.

My name is _____ (say your name)
My age at this moment in time is ____ (your age)
I live at _____in _____ (your residence address and city & state)

Now, take a moment and look around you. Notice the walls, the ceiling, the floor. Feel the floor under your feet. Touch your hair and the skin on your arms or hands. Get connected with your body sensations and areas in your body that feel tight. Slowly rotate your head around on your neck - first one way, then the other. Notice any crackling sounds - that is the air being released between your vertebrae. Breathe deeply as you do this.

Next say, *"I am standing (or sitting) and thinking about being alive in this moment. I am grateful to be here creating a future based on nothing - other than what I say I want."*

Chapter 6 (Cont'd)

Now consider this question:

Now that you are standing in the here and now, bring to your conscious mind what you have in your life that **you can easily see you are grateful for** and happy to have.

Then, bring to your conscious mind those things you have in your life that you may have forgotten you are grateful for and **choose to remember them and generate gratitude** for those things as well.

Finally, bring to your conscious mind those things you have in your life that you have resisted, have not wanted, or think are bad and wrong. Take a moment to see if you can find some value in having them or in having had them in the past. Once you do that, let your thoughts about them go. If you were unable to do that, it's fine - let that go as well.

Just be present to this moment; right now. Take a deep breath and notice your surroundings one more time.

Now: **Ask yourself one or more of the following questions,**
- ✓ "What do I want to create as a possible future?"
- ✓ "If I could have anything at all, what would it be?"
- ✓ "If I could be anywhere, where would I be?"
- ✓ What would be required of me to make that happen?

Chapter 6 (Cont'd)

You are now standing in the gap - between what is so - what is real in life right now **- and what you want to create** (a possibility). It can be an exhilarating, exciting, and sometimes scary place. And, it is a place that holds satisfaction, joy, fulfillment and many other things that make it worth getting up in the morning!

I invite you to consider that when you are really and truly present, you can see that the **only thing holding you back from having or being what you truly want to have or be in life is only YOU;** your thoughts and considerations from the past, your fears about your own abilities and your concern that you are not big enough or good enough to accomplish what you want.

And, I am here to tell you that you ARE big enough and smart enough and courageous enough if you stand in the present moment and take action on the field of life, instead of evaluating, judging and procrastinating from the sidelines.

So, as you stand in the gap... consider this question.

If you could be anything, do anything or have anything in your life, what would that be? Do you know? Can you imagine?

Chapter 6 (Cont'd)

For many of us, at some time in our lives, the answer may have been very clear and, depending on your age, where you are in your life right now, and where you intended to be, it is easy for you to bring that experience into clear focus. And, for others, the question may generate something like fear or a vacuum and what seems like a huge unknown. Pondering an uncertain future can feel disconcerting and can cause doubts and hesitancy about what is and is not possible to loom very large in that moment.

When we are young - under 30 - often our path stretches way out in front of us and it seems like there is all the time in the universe to decide where we are going and who we want to be in the world. The further on in life we get, the more focused some of us become on "what's next" or what we think "should" be next. Then, as we approach our middle years, it is easy to become impatient with the direction and/or lack of direction our lives have taken; seemingly without our having actually planned it that way.

Sometimes things and incidents get away from us and our progress seems random, unplanned, and ends up taking us in directions we never planned to go.

Regardless of where you are along that journey, taking the time at some point to create the conscious path for your existence - your purpose, for example - can make a difference in your ability to feel grounded and fruitful.

Chapter 6 (Cont'd)

I am going to invite you now to take some time to consider that as you stand in this moment - inside your consciously created "gap."

I am going to ask you, in this moment, standing in the "gap," to consider that you get to say what your life will be "in service of." That is, why you are here. It is a conversation you create with yourself and for yourself. No one else can have this conversation for you.

When you were a child, your parents did whatever they did to prepare you for this; yet, now, in this moment, you alone get to choose what you are here for and why you are alive and on the planet. You get to choose... in this moment. There is nowhere else to look, except inside your heart, to discover this answer.

You have reached the part of our conversation together where you will begin to create who you are - and what direction you will cause yourself to take. How that begins is with determining what touches, moves, and inspires you. It is about asking yourself some key questions and dwelling in the answers your heart gives you.

For most of the world's population, life can be expressed as a "survival" conversation. Many of us go through life hoping to survive the breakdowns, the challenges, the problems and, for many, the sometimes-devastating occurrences that can keep us stuck in life.

Chapter 6 (Cont'd)

What I am asking you to consider right now is that life is more than the challenges, problems and breakdowns with which each of us deal on a daily basis.

Life is about how we *handle those challenges and breakdowns.* Who are we in the face of those challenges problems and breakdowns - THAT is what determines the quality of our lives.

Now, we are going to look at one more possible conversation about "a gap."

This distinction was made clear to me in the transformational work I have done over the years – and I have seen its value, proven many times over as I experience life – and that is why I am sharing it with you, here.

The gap about which I am about to speak is better known as the **difference between those things we know, or think we know, and those things that are hidden from our view - our blind spots;** those undiscovered places in our lives where we are completely unaware of something and we are unaware that we cannot see them. In fact, even others may see something we are unable to see; either about ourselves or about life in general – yet it is completely hidden from us!

Chapter 6 (Cont'd)

As I've said before, that is because we each live our lives from our own perspective – it is the only one we have, after all. **I cannot see life through YOUR perspective because I am not looking through your eyes,** nor have I lived your experiences, no matter how close we might be. So, consequently, while I may have the ability to be compassionate, or empathetic about your life situation or current circumstances, I cannot really be in "your shoes."

Now, I may "study up" on what I think I should know about something, and gain knowledge about it, but there will still remain things that are "hidden from my view." Those could be said to be blind spots or things **I do not even know I do not know.**

So, that then, is another "gap" into which we are stepping now... An exploration of standing in what I think I already know, or what I think I need to learn – and a place where I am willing to be open to discovering my own blind spots – **or those things that I don't know I don't know; the discovery of which could alter my current way of being in life.**

Great possibilities can be created by standing in the "unknown" – in the willingness to be in the gap – and considering that there are things that, while they may threaten our "survival brain;" our limbic survival tool, they can also liberate our way of thinking.

Chapter 6 (Cont'd)

They can allow us to experience new, expansive ways of being; ways that are hard to explain, and yet, freeing beyond belief.

Ok – finally, here is the last thing I want to say about "Living into the Gap..."

Whether we thrive or survive - whether we live from our **limbic brain** or whether we **create life as a daring adventure**, is chosen by only one thing - US - and **the attitude** we bring to the game of life.

Soon, you are going to have the real opportunity to create that purpose for yourself and to design a new future to step into. We are going to explore your passions, your dreams and, that all important question - Why are you here and what is your purpose?

First, here is your **AffirmAction** for Chapter 6 and your follow up assignment that will prepare you for Chapter 7!

Get started now (and, remember, do not move ahead until it is complete!)

CHAPTER 6 – AFFIRMACTIONS & ASSIGNMENT

AFFIRM: Consider this. **You have just been born - there is nothing in your past and your amazing future lies in front of you.** What would you want to create as your first act tomorrow morning? With what statement would you start the day as you lie in bed, just before rising? It could be "Today I will make a huge difference for someone else so that THEY have the best day of their life!" or "The next 24 hours will be an AMAZING day and I will remain undaunted by anything that happens!" or "Today I will have the BEST day of my life" or "I will be empowered by everything that occurs in my life today" and journal that each day of this week.

Who will you BE and what will you say as you start this first day of the first week of the rest of your life?

ACTION: Consider what action you can take that would make a difference in the life of the first person you meet today. Take an action that can make that happen. This could be as little as giving a stranger a smile, or a friend a helping hand. This could be as much as loaning someone something they need to make their lives a little easier or it could mean reaching out to someone you have not spoken to in a long time and giving them an acknowledgement about the difference they have made in your life. Take an action that makes a difference for someone every day this week and at the end of the week, write in your journal how you feel about yourself and your life. Notice how your contribution to others has made a difference for you.

Chapter 6 (Cont'd)

Make a list of every job you have ever had in your life. List the things you loved about that job and the things you did not like about it. List at least ONE thing you loved. List at least one thing you learned from each job or position. What were the things you would want to continue doing if you could and what things would you never want to do again?

Make a list of each vacation or trip you have taken that gave you joy or taught you something valuable about yourself or others. Notice all the positive things that came out of those journeys.

Create a list of things others have told you that you do well and of things you really enjoy doing and that you think you do well.

What would you like to learn more about that you have been meaning to learn and have procrastinated about? What would it take for you to learn them? Who would you have to talk to about learning them or where would you have to go to learn those things?

What is missing for you that, if it was in place, you could gain that knowledge?

What are the skills you say you have that make you unique or that qualify you to contribute to others?

Chapter 6 (Cont'd)

What are the things you have avoided doing that will bring completion to an area of life that, right now, feels "incomplete?"

Standing in the "gap" between who you have been and who you are committed to being, what is missing that you believe would move you to the next level of accomplishment?

Who can support you in taking action in that direction?

Who will you contact in the next 12 hours to support you to do that?

If you could create, do, or say anything that would contribute to someone you love right now, what would that be? DO it!!

Congratulations on completing your assignment - **Now, on to Chapter 7!**

EMPOWERMENT CHAPTER 7

"A Survival Conversation – Need versus Want"

So, we have arrived at your next Chapter - Number 7; where we will examine further the nuances and distinctions of the Law of Attraction as well as a possible difference between spending our time "needing" something as opposed to wanting it.

First, let's consider this -

In exploring the dictionary's definition of Need...

As a noun...

Need is:

1. a requirement, necessary duty, or obligation
2. lack of something wanted or deemed necessary
3. necessity, arising from the circumstances of a situation or case
4. a condition marked by the lack of something requisite:
5. destitution; extreme poverty

As a verb...

Need is:

1. to be under an obligation or in a negative statement
2. to be in dire straits or missing something necessary for life

Chapter 7 (Cont'd)

Both forms of need indicate a severe lack of something and a negative experience attached to, and accompanied by, negative energy.

Now, let's consider Want and a definition of that word...

As a Noun...
Want is:
1. a desire or a demand for
2. the state of being without something which is desired
3. a lack of something demanded

As a Verb...
Want is:
1. to feel inclined toward something
2. to have something that would complete a condition for satisfaction
3. a preference of some kind for some thing, person or desired outcome

So, what am I getting at here?

To explain further, I will call into our conversation, a deeper exploration of the Law of Attraction, which I first mentioned earlier in this program.

Chapter 7 (Cont'd)

How exactly does the Law of Attraction work?

We talked, in Chapter 1, about **the Law of Attraction as** being, like gravity, a natural law of the universe. We told you that while you can't really see gravity at work, you CAN see the effect of it.

We asked you to consider that **some people attract a particular kind of "luck" to themselves** - and we said it had something to do with their "attitude" or way of being, right? We explained that supporters of the Law of Attraction would say that "bad luck" is the result of how people interact with the world around them and that the element of negativity "attracts" that kind of experience to them.

We recommended that you refrain from considering it as the "truth" - only that you "try it on" as a possible way that life works.

Especially since **we cannot SEE the Law of Attraction in action, and we can only speculate and examine the evidence that follows that speculation.** Finally, we asked that you take a few moments to examine those times in your life when you were particularly effective… and that you explore your **attitude at the time?**

Were you looking forward to success? Were you anticipating good things?

Chapter 7 (Cont'd)

We explained that proponents of the Law of Attraction would say that part of why you had "good things" come to you was because **your attitude was positive and that you created a clear intention rather than dwelling in negativity and what was not happening.**

So, now that we've reviewed the earlier statements we shared with you about it, let's delve a bit deeper into the scientific knowledge behind it...

Have you heard of "quantum physics"? It's something Einstein worked on along with myriad other mathematical geniuses and it is a fundamental branch of physics which deals with physical phenomena at a nanoscopic scale - way too complex for me to go into here.

However, having said that, this theory does impact each of us in a very real way and, according to proponents of the Law of Attraction, completely validates the belief that, quantum mechanics or physics, while abstract, **concretely impacts our daily lives.**

It has to do with energy; the fact that human beings are composed of energetic molecules causing the rules of "affinity" or natural attraction to come into play and has been explored and theorized over since the early 1600's.

Chapter 7 (Cont'd)

If we move forward to a more recent timeframe like the mid-20th century, social scientists began to more frequently reference and apply something called Plato's first law of "affinity;" which states that "like attracts like." This, they say, connects us with our desire - and our belief - that we have the ability to attract what we want in life based on the frequency of the "energy" output we generate.

Along with the Law of Attraction, there is another perspective as well; the **Law of Repulsion** - also built on the concept that we are all energy and that, depending on the frequency of that energy, we will either attract or push away that which we desire to have in our lives.

The premise being that we, as human beings constantly generating an energy field around us, have the ability to change the frequency of the energy flowing through us at any given time; from positive to negative, based on the thought patterns we choose through our unconscious thoughts and attitudes.

Simply put, when one monitors one's thoughts; consistently generating energy around how to have things work, generating gratitude and creating the presence of optimism, openness and relatedness with one's surroundings, the tendency of the energy that surrounds us is of attraction and positivity.

Chapter 7 (Cont'd)

On the other hand, when one is constantly on the lookout for danger, unworkability and the negative aspects of life, that, theoretically, generates a space of "negative" energy, a "pushing away" or repulsing that which is positive and beneficial in life.

So, after all is said and done, is this the TRUTH? Remember, what we said when we began this conversation; none of it is "true." We asked you to "try it on" and suppose that it could be accurate. If that is the case, what would be the best use of your thought processes? Looking for how to have life work or proving that it doesn't and that you are one of the "unlucky" ones in life.

I have found, that standing for attracting what I want and creating conversations for possibility are a great deal more satisfying and more likely to generate the kind of life experiences I want. Therefore, I am inviting you - Dear Reader - to embrace this new possibility for yourself.

For, if the *truth* be told, standing FOR a life of joy, fun, and ease certainly is more appealing than a life of strife, fear and loss. That is why I invite you to embrace the kind of energetic view that gratitude and workability can provide and to let go of negativity, worry and anxiety over circumstances you can probably not control.

Chapter 7 (Cont'd)

Now, you might be inclined at this juncture, to say "That is easier said than done," right? If you have had circumstances that cause you to say - for whatever reasons - that life has not shown up for you this way, and that it might be difficult for you to automatically come from a place of positivity right off the bat, I have good news!

With practice, you absolutely can accomplish this new way of looking at life. Yes, it requires practice. Yes, it requires being alert to your thoughts and automatic responses to negativity. It IS like building new habits. Simple, but not easy (and possible).

All that is required is a shift in attitude - along with an awareness and a clarity about where you are and where you want to be, rather than where you have been and the way it has always seemed in the past.

So, now that brings us to creating practices that can and will support us creating this kind of mindset and the ability to generate the kind of energy to which we are committed. **Positive, generative energy that delivers on the promise of a life of joy, satisfaction and fulfillment.**

Shall we begin?

Great.

Chapter 7 (Cont'd)

Here is an exercise to begin the process. It is helpful if you can do this with someone else. Someone who will refrain from judgment and **who is willing to do the same exercise with you.**

Take out several single, lined, clean pieces of paper. At the top of the first one, label it "Negativity" or "My Negative Mind." Write down all the negative things the voice in your head is saying right now or has said in the past - let them all flow out through your pen onto the paper in front of you. All the what-ifs, how-abouts, whys, why nots, and all the negativity you have experienced in the past or are experiencing now. Get it all written down - leave nothing unsaid. Take as much time as you need to do that now. Allow all the negativity you have inside to be expressed here.

Include all the reasons you have to be negative; everything you don't have that you want, all the bad things you think are "personal" to you; things others would not understand or that you have encountered as a result of what others think and do.

Write until there is nothing more to write. This could take a while so be thorough. Get it all said. If you need more paper, get it and keep going until there is nothing more to say.

Begin now…

Chapter 7 (Cont'd)

_____

_____

_____

_____

_____

_____

_____

_____

_____

_____

_____

_____

_____

_____

_____

_____

_____

_____

_____

_____

_____

_____

_____

_____

_____

Chapter 7 (Cont'd)

_____

_____

_____

_____

_____

_____

_____

_____

_____

_____

_____

_____

_____

_____

_____

_____

_____

_____

_____

_____

_____

_____

Chapter 7 (Cont'd)

_____

_____

_____

_____

_____

_____

_____

_____

When you are finished writing. Read it silently to yourself. See if you left anything out and if you did, add it. Now, read this document silently to yourself again and make sure it is complete.

Next, read your document to your friend and give yourself some freedom to really allow yourself to experience all the negativity, any anger, upset or annoyances this information gives you. Ask your partner if they get your upset and communication about these things.

Notice if there is anything still there for you - any charge or upset around any of the issues. If there are, read the entire document again. Read it until you have no charge on anything you have written and you are "clear" that you never again have to deal with that issue or upset.

Chapter 7 (Cont'd)

Explain to your friend to do the same.

You will be amazed that, for the most part, these negative experiences will no longer have a charge for you. **If they do - you are not complete with the issue. Begin again!**

Now... on to what's next; that is, after the negativity has lost some of its grip on who you are in this moment. Well, consider that there are, essentially, two things you can concentrate on - what is not working in your life and what IS working. Since we have now addressed our almost constant addiction to what is NOT working, and the negativity that often dominates our thoughts and, therefore, our actions, let's now look at something you could call "signs of land."

What possibly could that mean - "Signs of Land?"

Well, assume you have been stranded on a boat for days - you are a castoff in a body of water, desperately looking for - what? You guessed it - Signs of Land, right? Signs that somewhere, hopefully close by, there is land and salvation from a deep watery grave!

Now, what would a sign of land look like to someone adrift in a vast expanse of water? Perhaps a branch floating by? A leaf? A turtle on a rock? Even a bird gives some indication of land somewhere close.

Chapter 7 (Cont'd)

Those, for a sailor adrift, would definitely be signs of land.

Likewise, for someone waiting for a change in their life, for some sign of success or of a dream becoming reality, what would appear as a "sign of land?"

Let's look at one example in particular.

I have a friend - one who has been longing for many years to find that "special" someone - the man of her dreams. **Yet, he never seems to appear.** And, every time she goes out with a new potential suitor, she comes home disappointed and discouraged.

For example:
Date number 1 - "Well," she'll say, "he started out as a good potential date; had a great sense of humor, but then I noticed how grimy his fingernails were (he's a mechanic) and how messy and dirty his hair seemed - clearly not someone I could possibly care for in the long run."

Date number 2 - "I really thought he would be the one. He's smart and a great conversationalist, but short and bald -AND, to top it off, he had bad breath. I could just never love a bald man."

Chapter 7 (Cont'd)

Date number 3 - "Nice guy, yes - AND intelligent with a good sense of humor. BUT, he could not dance worth a darn and I am definitely committed to being with a man who has rhythm and can dance well - so he's definitely NOT the one."

Ok - get the picture. **This is NOT someone looking for "signs of land."** More like someone looking for reasons why she will probably never find the person she is looking so desperately to find.

On the other hand, someone who IS looking for signs of land might be more likely to have a conversation like this...

Date number 1 - "Well," she'd say, "that was a delightful evening and although he probably isn't the person I want to spend my life with, he did have a great sense of humor and we spent a lovely evening laughing and enjoying each other's company. He's also a great mechanic and will be the perfect person to help me if I have difficulty finding a new car. He definitely confirmed for me that there are men out there who can laugh at themselves and at life's mishaps and that friendship with someone like him is a definite plus."

Date number 2 - "This guy was so interesting - a great conversationalist - and someone that would be a wonderful friend.

Chapter 7 (Cont'd)

I think he may need some dental work; however, not until I know him better would I say anything. In the meantime, I offered him a mint and we talked about dance lessons since he really wants to learn how to dance. We both agreed that would be a great way to meet other people as well - for him AND for me and we're going to look into it."

Date number 3 - "I am getting more and more encouraged about my finding the perfect guy. After all, I have already met someone with a great sense of humor, someone who likes to converse on all kinds of interesting subjects and someone interested in learning to dance. All in all, it's clear to me that I am getting closer and closer to someone who will be a perfect match and I'm having fun and making great friends doing it!"

THIS **is someone *looking* for signs of land -** and someone who is much more likely to find that perfect guy because where she is looking is at what **IS** working, what **DOES show up** as a possibility instead of what isn't working and why she is failing to find her dream partner in life.

So... working definition? Looking for signs of land is a way of looking for what works!

Chapter 7 (Cont'd)

Enjoying the present moment instead of always experiencing disappointment in current circumstances - experiencing failure and disappointment and never stopping to explore the advantages and opportunities that they encounter along the path to fulfillment.

This, then, is what you could say is a basic tenant of the Law of Attraction... **What you focus on will tend to attract what you get; focus on negative, you will get negativity - focus on what is working and positive in your life, and it will be naturally drawn to you**. Because human beings are comprised of energetic molecules, and "like" subatomic particles attract the same, the naturally occurring state of the Universe will tend toward delivering that which you concentrate upon. Like gravity, you may not "see" it - however, you will experience it - to that, millions of human beings will attest, and I am one of them.

Moving on, in this really key Empowerment Chapter, what we'd like to look at next is something critical to causing breakthroughs and wanted results in your life - and that is the empowering subject of TRUST.

Consider this ...

Have you heard or experienced this kind of an interaction between a parent and a child?

Chapter 7 (Cont'd)

Child: I don't like my teacher; she says mean things to me.
Mother: I'm sure your teacher is not really being mean. You probably just did something that wasn't nice. If you behave, she will not say mean things.

Parent: Go give your Uncle Harold a hug, Susie.
Child: I don't want to - I don't like Uncle Harold; he's creepy.
Parent: Don't you dare say things like that. Of course, you like him - he's your uncle. Now go give him a hug.

Child: Mom, why are you angry with me?
Parent: I'm not angry - don't be silly. Now, go play outside.

Mother: It's cold out; put on a sweater.
Child: I'm not cold - I don't need a sweater.
Mother: Yes, you do. You're just a kid and don't know what you need. Listen to me, I'm your mother, I know best; put on a sweater if you're going out.

Child: I'm afraid to sleep without a light.
Father: Don't be silly - there's nothing to be afraid of. Go to sleep right now; you don't need a light.

Chapter 7 (Cont'd)

After being told as children, time after time, not to trust our own feelings; after being told we must give others the power to determine what our experience of life should be, it is little wonder that as we mature, our trust of ourselves and of our sometimes valid, intuitive experiences can begin to erode that trust. **We learn, sometimes in very small and subtle ways, to discount and mistrust our feelings,** deciding that others must know better than we about what we should feel and understand.

So, even though we can often feel in our gut what is true and what is untrue, many of us don't listen to these inner messages. Instead, we put our trust in others and then feel betrayed and justified in not trusting others when they often let us down.

Learning to develop a consistent inner trust; a "bonding" with ourselves and our intuition, can help us in becoming a trust "worthy" adult. Consider then, the theory that trusting others begins by trusting our Self.

You can begin this process by noticing how many times a week you promise yourself you will do something. It can be one of many things - check out the following list and see how many of them you have promised to do - and then failed to follow up with them…

Let's begin with one of my favorites… Working out!

Chapter 7 (Cont'd)

You promise yourself that you will...

- ✓ Work out on a regular basis
- ✓ Be on time for meetings
- ✓ Drink less soda
- ✓ Eat less red meat
- ✓ Take time to meditate
- ✓ Get more sleep
- ✓ Clean up clutter or the house
- ✓ Finish a project,
- ✓ Lose weight
- ✓ Call that friend or relative you have been avoiding for months
- ✓ or even just spend time taking care of yourself?

Here's a quick assignment: Add to this list anything you have been saying you would do and have not done.

- _____
  _____
- _____
  _____
- _____
  _____
- _____
  _____
- _____

Chapter 7 (Cont'd)

It is possible that when you fail to keep your word to yourself, you begin to experience a higher level of distrust - and that distrust of yourself is what sets the stage for how you interact with the world around you. **Build trust in yourself and you will begin to see that trust reflected back to you by others in your life.**

It's the beginning of creating trust among friends and relationships - and extends even to your community and, ultimately, as you know, trust is a global conversation. It all begins with you.

And now, neophyte to the world of transformation, here is a cautionary word…

Be careful lest you begin to feel "righteous" about how you are keeping your word to yourself, therefore others should do the same. Notice if you are judging others by your actions - this never works. We can only change ourselves - never anyone else. Only THEY can change or transform themselves and only when they have chosen to do so.

It might be wise here to take a moment to recall our conversation about taking responsibility for everything in our lives; our relationships, our interactions with others in the community and our global footprint. Only when WE begin to take 100% responsibility for ourselves and for what we do - Only when we begin to take 100% responsibility for what others do to us and (third level coming up…) what others do to others, can we begin to shift   reality.

Chapter 7 (Cont'd)

Not because it is the "truth" that we are responsible for what others do to others - only because when WE are the source of who we are, what we do and what we have, can anything alter.

And so it goes with trust; only when we take 100% responsibility for creating trust between ourselves and our world, will the world begin to reflect back that trust to us.

On that note, let's begin to wrap up Empowerment Chapter 7 with our AffirmActions and assignment.

Remember, do not move forward until you have completed this chapter's assignment.

Cheers!

> "Only the truth of who you are, if realized, will set you free."
>
> Eckhart Tolle
>
> "This above all: To thine own self be true,
> And it must follow as the night the day
> Thou canst not then be false to any man.""
>
> Shakespeare (Hamlet)

CHAPTER 7 AFFIRMACTIONS & ASSIGNMENT

AFFIRM: At the end of every day this week, before going to bed, notice and make a list of those things that occurred in your day that - at first – showed up as negative (or what seemed to be bad news, unlucky, or a negative circumstance). Now examine that "happening" or occasion from a different perspective. Explore what in that circumstance or situation could have the potential for something good to come out of it. What kind of benefits could be gained by you having suffered that loss or that unfortunate occasion? Is there anything at all that you can see would have that - ultimately - turn out to be beneficial for you or for someone else?

Think to yourself, "The negativity of this situation could be in my perspective of looking at it. If I shift my view, I can see that... (here you can reframe and restate to yourself the possible benefits for that circumstance to have occurred), I could see things differently.

ACTION: Write a note to yourself about what you have seen as a result of changing your Point of View (POV) about this situation or circumstance - and then look to see if there are any actions you can now take as a result of that way of thinking that could alter the current circumstances in reality.

Let's put you in the scenario of something that happened to a friend of mine: You were walking around late at night, making last minute arrangements for a morning athletic event you had been planning for weeks.

Chapter 7 (Cont'd)

You did not turn on the light because you knew where everything you wanted was and did not want to disturb others in the family who were sleeping.

You decided to make a quick trip to the closet to get your athletic bag ready so you could be on time in the morning and catch a few extra winks of sleep, and suddenly, BAM! You stub your toe in the dark - REALLY hard. *"Owww, holy cow &*!!*&%\$#/!!??*&!!"* You are hurt, *angry, in pain...* and when you look down at your toes, you can see that they are really damaged - fast turning blue and swelling up like little sausages! Clearly, something has been broken - either a blood vessel or a bone - or both so you run to grab some ice to mitigate the damage.

Now, sitting down in the dark, the tears begin to flow - and not just from the pain. It's very clear already - that event tomorrow? Not gonna happen! That thing you have been training for, looking forward to, bragging about that you were going to "nail it" - it's history. You are out of the game; period. The anger and upset are overwhelming and it seems like such a pointless loss.

So, of course, the first tendency is anger - upset - recriminations. Why didn't you turn on the light, what was that stupid planter doing there in the first place, who moved it?! Why weren't you more careful?! Why so clumsy? You get the picture, right?

Chapter 7 (Cont'd)

Now, what if, in that moment in time - you stopped and said to yourself...

"Ok, it's happened. I will not be able to perform tomorrow. Period, end of story. There is nothing I can do about it now other than make sure I clean up the wound and ice and elevate my foot until I can get to the doctor.

So, what good could come out of this miserable experience?
Well, there is someone on the team who has been wanting to excel but has not had the opportunity to move ahead in the rankings. I could spend a few minutes tomorrow giving them some coaching on something I have learned that has really helped me improve. Also, I have been meaning to meditate for many years, and have never taken the time to learn that - so this week, when I clearly will not be able to participate in much physical activity, I could clearly take at least a few hours to learn meditation and use it to empower my future wellbeing.

Finally, I could spend the time this week reading that book that I have been meaning to read - and which I have been avoiding because I have been spending so much time working out my body rather than relaxing and enjoying my free time off from work."

Chapter 7 (Cont'd)

Of course, none of this changes the fact that you cannot participate in the event; however, you can see the difference your attitude can make in your state of mind - and, consequently, in the state of mind of others around you - people who share your world.

What is better for others to experience - a friend or family member who is upset, angry, and punishing themselves and everyone else for an accident, or someone who is using the occasion to empower someone else and take care of themselves; taking advantage of the opportunity to expand their way of looking at life and exploring the new paths that opened up as a result of an unfortunate incident?

On to your second "AffirmAction" for Chapter 7...

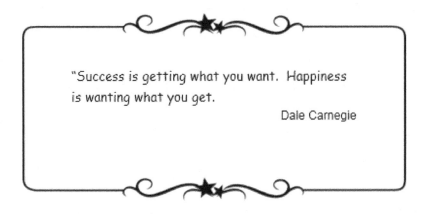

"Success is getting what you want. Happiness is wanting what you get.
                              Dale Carnegie

Chapter 7 (Cont'd)

AFFIRM: Notice as you go through your week any "intuitive nudges" you experience. Begin to be awake to nuances in your experiences of others and whether you are feeling more trusting of situations in which you find yourself on a daily basis. You can, of course, create your own affirmation about trusting yourself and others. Here is one example of an affirmation you could try on: "I am a trustworthy human being and I attract others who are trustworthy into my life. I do what I say I will do when I say I will do it - and, if I don't, I am responsible to clean it up with anyone who is inconvenienced by my failing to keep my word either to myself or others."

ACTION: This is a simple one. Each day, make a list of at least one thing you have been meaning to do from the list in the Chapter above or anything you added to that list. Do one thing each day and complete it. At the end of the day, check it off your list and acknowledge yourself for having kept your word. **If you do not do what you said you would do, do not punish or berate yourself in any way.** Acknowledge what you did and did not do. Make no excuses; just clean it up and resolve to take action on it the next day; then just do it!

Have fun with your assignment!

Now off to **Empowerment Chapter 8**

"Cherish your visions and your dreams as they are the children of your soul, the blueprints of your ultimate achievements."

Napoleon Hill

"If you don't like something, change it. If you can't change it, change your attitude."

Maya Angelou

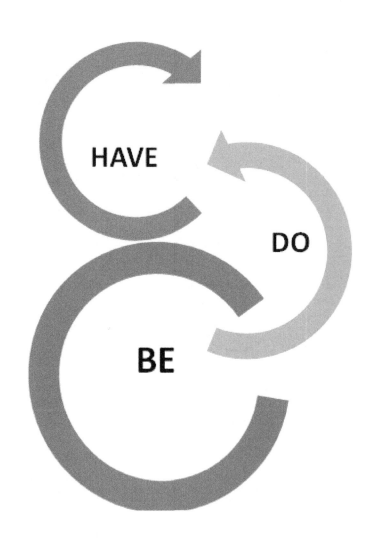

EMPOWERMENT CHAPTER 8

Be-Do-Have in Depth

As you may have noticed, the title of this book - includes and, indeed, prominently features the word "being" - and not by mistake. As shared earlier, we explored a conversation about the way most of us experience being in life - the ordinary, inherited way of being or, said differently, the way in which it seems that life has unfolded for us. That is, we need to DO a certain thing in order to HAVE or get what we want, and then, *finally*, we can we BE who we want to be.

We have asked you to consider that there is an alternative; a more powerful way of being - a way to "be" in life so that things can come more easily and so that we can accomplish more of what we are up to. That way is to turn the formula - the ordinary, Do-Have-Be, way of living around and, instead, operate in a BE-Do-Have world.

In other words, begin by BEING who you want to be, and then what you need to do will naturally call to you out of who you are **being**; it will make the appropriate actions very clear - you will know what you are required to DO and finally, you will HAVE what you want to have out of already being who you want to be.

Chapter 8 (Cont'd)

Being **something or some way is a "created" state of mind**; it is not the default mode in which we generally operate.

Let's look at an example.

If you love music - and you are studying hard to become a wonderful musician. You are doing all the right things, practicing in all your spare time, playing whenever you can, listening to great music - but somehow, becoming a great musician has eluded you.

You still have not taken that great "leap of faith" and become the musician you long to be. We would say you are living a "Do-Have-Be" life.

For most of us, that IS the way it is in life. And so, we struggle, day by day, to create the kind of life or way of "being" that would satisfy us or bring us fulfillment.

Now, consider for a moment, that while that IS one way of living, there is actually another, more satisfying and more effective way of living.

What if, for example, you began living life **from an exploration of your way of being** instead of what you were doing?

Chapter 8 (Cont'd)

What if you created a "Be-Do-Have" life rather than a "Do-have-be" life?

Look; If who you are BEING is a musician, what is the first thing you do when you get up in the morning? Your entire being is that of a musician, so what actions would you be called to take - what would you DO each and every moment and each and every day? You would be immersing yourself in music, wouldn't you? Meeting musicians, going to classes, listening to music and practicing every spare moment, talking to people about music, studying and finding ways to play music...

You would think like a musician; truly living the existence of a musician; and, you would be called to take all the actions a musician would take. You would then have the results a musician would have - people would be looking at you and speaking to you as they would speak to a musician because that is who you are BEING.

And, as a consequence of who you are being, and what you are doing, you would soon have that music career that you longed for... but ONLY when you begin with being willing to have that occur. Until then, you are just working at, trying, striving for - and just missing - the boat, because only when you come FROM *being* a musician does the experience - and distinction - musician – arise.

Chapter 8 (Cont'd)

As an artist, your experience would be similar. If who you are *being* is an artist, then the actions to take - on a daily basis - will occur to you naturally out of who you are being in your life - as an artist.

So, let's talk a little bit more about this experience of beginning that "Be-Do-Have" existence today.

First, you need to be clear about what – or rather who – it is you really want to "be." Let's assume for the moment, all your "doing" is done and you already ARE what you wanted to be, what is that? Take a few minutes to think about it and explore your thoughts by writing them below.

Who would you choose to be? Be as specific as possible – describe it as you see it visualize it in great detail.

_____

_____

_____

_____

_____

_____

_____

_____

_____

Chapter 8 (Cont'd)

Next, imagine what your life would be like **if you were being who you chose to be**, right now? What would you be wearing, where would you be going, who would you be with and what would your life look like if you were being who you wanted to be?

Only once you are clear who or what you are being and what it would feel like, can you then begin to see what you would be doing or having as a result of who you were being.

If you are clear who or how you are being (and ONLY then), describe what you would be doing and what you would have... Write that below. Really let yourself experience having and doing all that being who you are would allow.

_____

_____

_____

_____

_____

_____

_____

_____

_____

_____

_____

Chapter 8 (Cont'd)

_____

_____

_____

_____

_____

_____

_____

_____

_____

_____

Creating your life in this way takes practice. You have been living a Do-Have-Be life for a long time. Creating a Be-Do-Have life requires work – the work of transformation – the work of "BEING in this moment and creating the future you want from the present.

Take your time – Think about what your AffirmActions for this week will look like. You will be creating them from being who you want to be for the future you want to have.

Now, move on to your AffirmActions and Assignment for Chapter 8.

CHAPTER 8 - AFFIRMACTIONS & ASSIGNMENT

AFFIRM: Create your Affirmations this week from your new paradigm, Be-Do-Have. When you get up each morning, create who you are being for the day and then live FROM that way of being. It will call you into action.

_____

_____

_____

_____

_____

_____

_____

_____

_____

ACTION: Make note below of the actions you will take each day connected with who you are being. Remember, this takes diligent practice. After all, you are overcoming the habits of a lifetime and it will take great courage, stamina, and determination to create that new way of being each day.

_____

_____

_____

_____

_____

_____

Chapter 8 (Cont'd)

_____

_____

_____

_____

_____

Notice when you succeed and your experience of it – AND, notice when you fail and become a human "doing" because you are no longer in touch with who you are being.

Remember, there are no mistakes – it will take time and practice to change the patterns of a lifetime.

ASSIGNMENT FOR CHAPTER 8

Make a list of all the ways you would be "being" different if you were being the person you wanted to be.

What would you focus on?

How would you treat yourself?

How would you look at finances differently than you have in the past?

What would your relationships be like?

Would you have different relationships?

Chapter 8 (Cont'd)

Explore all these different aspects of how your life would be different if you were "being" who you wanted and INTEND to be?

ASSIGNMENT:

_____

_____

_____

_____

_____

_____

_____

_____

_____

_____

_____

_____

_____

_____

_____

_____

_____

_____

_____

_____

Chapter 8 (Cont'd)

Be aware this week of consciously creating your way of "being" in the moment: For example, who is it important for me to be at this moment? If I was that person, what would my experience of life be at this moment? What would I be feeling? How would I be acting? If I had already achieved the goal of who I say I want to be, what would I be doing?

Remember, you must start with already being that person you say you want to be. Happy, artistic, a success at business, a writer, a musician, entrepreneur, chef? Out of being or coming from being that, the appropriate actions will show up to make that real in the world so that you can have all those things that you have dreamed you would have. **Begin right now!**

*(**Pssst**... Remember to look for signs of land!)*

EMPOWERMENT CHAPTER 9

Be "Here & Now" and Let Everything Else Go!

"Holding on to resentment is like taking poison and hoping someone else will die"

Buddha

This quote has been attributed to many people (However, whoever said it, hit the nail on the head, so I am going to use it anyway!). If I tell you to live in the moment and to "let go" of the past - past resentments, regrets, upsets, opinions, grudges, and anger, what does your "mind" tell you?

(Hint: Remember we talked about this in Chapter 5 – being present?)

It could range from "Oh, sure, what does SHE know about my upsets, regrets, experiences, or even anything about what my life has been for the past (number here) of years? Nothing!" and, you would be right! I DO know nothing about YOUR life or anything else about what has occurred for you in the past. What I do know, however, is that right now, in this moment, there IS no past. It exists only in YOUR memory - only in what YOU say about it - Only in the mind.

Chapter 9 (Cont'd)

All there is RIGHT now is right now - or, as Werner once said "successive moments of NOW, and now, and now, and now...

When we talked about the past, present, and future earlier in the book, we looked at how we live our lives mostly in the past, ignoring the only time we really have, in the moment - in the successive moments of NOW. **Life comes at us with urgency in THIS moment - not in the past (which is gone) and not in the future (which has not arrived) - only in the now.**

So why, if there is no past and no future - ready for us to walk into - why, Good Reader, would we hold onto resentments and regrets from that non-existent past?

Can we learn from the past - absolutely!

Can we be informed by the past in making decisions in the present - positively!

AND, we can still be present in this moment, forsaking the automatic "dwelling" in the past, literally "letting go" of anything that ties us to the past - and step forward into a future we create from...dare I say it? A future created from nothing! A clear space that exists only - where? In the PRESENT!

Chapter 9 (Cont'd)

More about creating the future standing in the present in our final
Empowerment Chapter, coming next.

For now, we are merely practicing "letting go" and, for that, here are a
few excellent activities designed to "**exorcise**" (look it up in your
WikkyWhatever dictionary) the past. Try them on...

"When I let go of what I am, I become what I might be.
When I let go of what I have, I receive what I need."

Tao Te Ching

Chapter 9 (Cont'd)

Make it your practice to begin each day with an exercise of being present.

Here are several suggestions.

They can all be done standing up or sitting down – at any place or time of the day. The only thing required is to "be still" and focus on your breath

1. Begin by noticing your breath as you breathe out and then in slowly. Each breathing cycle should last for approximately 6 seconds. Breathe in through your nose and out through your mouth.

Let go of your thoughts as you breathe – just watch them go by. Simply allow yourself to be still and focus your senses on your breathing. Picture your breath as it travels its pathway through your body and its energy flows out into the world.

2. Mindful Awareness

As you go through your day, take a moment to notice something that happens each day; for example, opening or closing a door. Notice the moment you touch the handle; stop and experience how you feel in that moment; the texture of the door handle, the room you are entering and the floor beneath your feet. Notice if there is a change of texture on the floor from one room to the (tile to carpet or carpet to wood

Chapter 9 (Cont'd)

How do you feel in that moment, when you are passing from one room to another? Is the smell or the air temperature different? Be mindful – Take a moment to turn off auto-pilot and consciously choose to appreciate where you are in the moment.

3. Observe your surroundings

Take a moment to notice a natural object in your immediate area; a bird, a flower, a stone, or the sky. Just be with whatever you are observing. Visually explore every aspect of its form. Relax into the harmony of nature and connect to it for as long as you are comfortable. Observe it as if for the first time and do nothing other than observe this one thing. This is especially helpful if you find yourself rushing around, shopping, getting errands done and experiencing the pressures of a busy day.

4. Mindful Listening

Turn on the radio – stop on the first station with music you come to. Listen to a piece of music you have never listened to before. Avoid judging the genre of the music, the style or rhythm, and be with whatever has turned up when you turned on the radio. Allow yourself to fully be with what is playing, letting go of judgment, evaluation and opinion as to whether you like it or not. Give your awareness permission to just be with whatever the music is sharing with you. *The idea is just to listen to the composition without preconception or judgment of the lyrics, the artist or the instrumental style.*

Chapter 9 (Cont'd)

5. Activity Mindfulness

Take on a routine task; mowing the lawn, cleaning the bathroom or kitchen, making the bed; something you typically do on an ordinary day. Create it as a new experience, noticing every nuance, every action you take to accomplish the task. Take each action consciously and experience each motion and movement as if you have never done it before.

Really BE with the activity and notice your thoughts – let them be – and continue until you are complete. Do not rush to get on with something else. Be with the task as an exercise in mindfulness.

6. Appreciation

Notice 6 things in your day that typically go unnoticed and underappreciated. Whether it is a person or an object, take the time to acknowledge to yourself the value and/or appreciation you have for this item or person.

Some examples could be, the mailman and the mail that arrives in your mailbox nearly every day with little or no effort on your part. The flowers that grow along the highway, or the birds that are singing outside your house in the morning when you go out to walk the dog. Maybe it is the hot water that comes from your tap when you are ready to shower, without you having to get out a kettle and boil it, the electricity that runs through the wires outside your home that allows you to have light in the evening.

Chapter 9 (Cont'd)

Here's a way to integrate what we learned in Chapter 8 – Be-Do-Have – and Be Here Now: Give it a try...

Take a few minutes in the beginning of the day to get a clear picture of how you want to be *being* as you go through your day.

Sit quietly and create being it in your mind. Is it "contented?" "satisfied?" "creative?"

Next, focus your thoughts on what your life will be like today if you are being that. Use all of your senses to imagine this state of being. How will you feel, what will you hear and see? Fully imagine this and allow yourself to experience it.

Finally, as that way of being, **what actions could you be taking or what would you be doing today** that is in sync with who you are being?

Imagine doing that and then be aware as you do it what your experience is and how you feel. If you can begin to practice this each day, more and more you will begin to live in this moment, creating your future from who you are being and living in this moment as you create your future.

Chapter 9 (Cont'd)

Once you realize at a gut level that while you "have" thoughts, you are not those thoughts, you can begin to tame your "monkey mind" (a favorite expression of many of my Buddhist friends) … you know, the thoughts that jump from one thing to another – like monkeys jumping through the tree tops – you can begin to be present in THIS moment.

Too often, our minds are thinking (**"WE" are not**) of the past, recent upsets, coming vacations or responsibilities we must fulfill, work we have left undone, or relationships we must rehabilitate "one of these days." While those thoughts occupy our mind – and our time - we are losing the present moment – we are missing what is currently occurring in our world, in the moments around us and we are failing to "be here now."

Living in THIS moment is our opportunity for truly being mindful, present, available to life. Focusing on the present moment provides many gifts and, while it takes practice, that practice leads to rich rewards. When you savor the moment, you avoid worrying about the future, about how you will look to others, about your doubts and fears from the past and for the future.

Have you ever visited a place so beautiful, that your first words were "Oh, it is so beautiful here – I can't wait to come back!" when in actuality – here you are now, in this moment?

Chapter 9 (Cont'd)

Yet, here you are, taken with the mind chatter about coming back "some other day," losing the joy of this very moment in the hoping for something else in a future that does not yet exist.

We are crazy, right?

We eat a delicious meal and compare it to one we had yesterday or will have tomorrow; we worry as we eat our favorite ice-cream that it has so many calories we will have to diet tomorrow, failing to be with the joy of the moment.

And now, here is a brilliant quote on all of this from an article by Jan Dixit, called the *Art of Now*:

"The most fundamental paradox of all is that Mindfulness isn't a goal, because goals are about the future, but you do have to set the intention of paying attention to what's happening at the present moment. As you read the words printed on this page, as your eyes distinguish the black squiggles on white paper, as you feel gravity anchoring you to the planet, wake up!

Become aware of being alive. And breathe.

As you draw your next breath, focus on the rise of your abdomen on the in-breath, the stream of heat through your nostrils on the out-breath.

Chapter 9 (Cont'd)

If you're aware of that feeling right now, as you're reading this, you're living in the moment. Nothing happens next. It's not a destination. This is it. You're already there!"

Thank you, Jan - *We got it!*

"The only time you ever have in which to learn anything or see anything or feel anything, or express any feeling or emotion, or respond to an event, or grow, or heal, is this moment, because this is the only moment any of us ever gets. You're only here now, you're only alive in this moment."

Jon Kabat-Zinn

CHAPTER 9 - AFFIRMACTIONS & ASSIGNMENT

AFFIRM: I have a past and I do not come from the past. I own the past and everything in it. I take responsibility for the past and all that I created in the past. I let go of blame, fault, regret, and resentment about the past; from the deeds of others and the deeds of my own. The past exists only in the conversations I have about it and I am letting go of negative conversations about the past and my connection to them. I will live consciously, in the present, and when I find myself drawn into the past and experiencing anger, resentment or blame, I will remember an anonymous quote I once heard…

"Never let the past spoil your present or govern your future."

With it, I remind myself that the past is gone and exists only in what I say about it, keeping it alive.

The only memories from the past that I willingly keep alive are those that give me joy, happiness and connect me with love. The rest I let go of - sending them into the void.

ACTION: Create an awareness each day of being in the moment and notice when you are not - then let go of those thoughts. One good way to do that is to get into an action; use your body to perform a good deed or acknowledge someone for the difference they have made in your life or in the lives of others.

Chapter 9 (Cont'd)

Next Assignment:

Look for signs of land whenever you are out and about - signs that things are going well for you and that good things are bound to follow.

Remember to take the time at the end of each day to make a list of all that you are grateful for; of everything good that occurred during the day - either to you or someone else you care about.

Repeat this statement to yourself whenever needed:

"I release resentments, regrets, judgments, evaluations & indictments of myself and others. I love my life, I celebrate every moment I am alive, and I flourish when I am present to life in this moment."

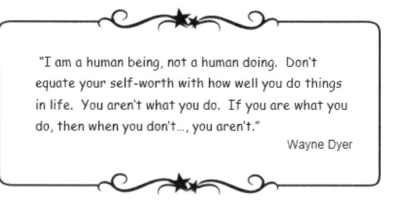

"I am a human being, not a human doing. Don't equate your self-worth with how well you do things in life. You aren't what you do. If you are what you do, then when you don't..., you aren't."

Wayne Dyer

EMPOWERMENT CHAPTER 10

The End is the Beginning

Design Your Present by Standing in Your Created Future

So, Dear Reader, as you approach the end of your Book of Being...
What is it you will have gained from having read it?

Are you being more present? Have you gained a sense of freedom
from the past?

What has the program provided for you that was missing before and
how will you implement what you have learned from its AffirmActions
as you move into your future?

Can you see a path to create a new and different future than you had
imagined? And, what does that title mean: Design your Present by
Standing in Your Created Future? That sounds pretty weird, doesn't
it?

Let me explain.

Chapter 10 (Cont'd)

If you've ever taken on a project - and set out dates and times, accompanied by milestones, you may understand how daunting a process that can be. Without knowing what you will encounter along the way and trying to "figure out" what you need to do to get to the next level of a project's completion when beginning from scratch can be a real challenge.

Let's look - from a different perspective - at another way to approach creating that new future.

First, consider this.

For the most part, what human beings do when asked what they want to accomplish in their future is **that they look to the past**; at what they have already accomplished or failed to accomplish.

They look at their limitations and their past skill sets; at their old feelings, past history of failures, wins and losses. Then, based on evidence of what their past says they can - or cannot - do, or what they have been capable of doing or incapable of doing (in the past) they begin to create what they think is their future.

Chapter 10 (Cont'd)

This provides an extremely limited view and, really, can only bring you more of the past.

Actually, what you are doing is examining the past and CALLING it your future. You will have taken past limitations, skills and beliefs, held them up in front of you and walked into them once again; calling THAT your created future. You could say that would be more about "re-creating the past" than designing a new future.

That is why, for our purposes here, I am going to ask you to consider this, a new way of perceiving the future.

Consider that the only way to truly create the future is to stand in the present, fully here - with no past limitations; explore your desires, your interests and your commitment to your purpose or mission in life, and THEN, looking at that, create a new future, based on nothing other than possibility.

You might ask, **"How can I do that?"**

Well, the first thing to do is to commit to getting clear about what you want to have in your life –

Chapter 10 (Cont'd)

What IS your purpose or why are you here and where do you want to be by a certain time? [Five years from now could be a good place to begin]

Consider all the work we have been doing up until now in our Book of Being. What have you discovered about "being" human? About ontology? About the distinctions between want and need? What about everything you have gotten complete with as you moved through these chapters?

Creating a future that leaves the past behind and has you be fully in the present with no baggage from that past, will require a whole new way of thinking - a transformed way of looking at your life.

Where better to begin that than here?

In order to begin the process, first engage in the following exercise. It will take you through the steps of discovering your purpose - or as some people call it, your mission - and then I will provide a second exercise where you will begin to create your future, standing in that discovered personal purpose or mission.

Chapter 10 (Cont'd)

Let's begin by reading the following quote...

On Commitment

Until one is committed,
There is hesitancy, the chance to draw back,
Always ineffectiveness.

Concerning all acts of initiative (and creation),
There is one elementary truth
The ignorance of which kills countless ideas and splendid plans:

That the moment one definitely commits oneself,
Then Providence moves too.

All sorts of things occur to help one
That would never otherwise have occurred.

A whole stream of events issue from the decision,
Raising in one's favor all manner of unforeseen
Incidents and meetings and material assistance,
Which no man could have dreamed would have come his way.

Whatever you can do or dream you can, begin it.
Boldness has genius, magic, and power in it.

Chapter 10 (Cont'd)

[**Note:** Literature tells us that this quote has erroneously been attributed to the German philosopher Goethe, when, in reality it was first spoken by W.H. Murray in Scottish Himalaya Expedition, 1951]

First Exercise: How to invent and discover your purpose/mission:

Let's begin with a few questions about your life...

STEP 1: Mark these from 1 to 5 – [1 = Absolutely NOT and 5 = Yes].

☐ Do you feel passionate about the work or activities you are doing in life?

☐ Do you know what inspiration is and do you let it guide you in life?

☐ Do you feel you are contributing to something greater in life than yourself?

☐ If you could do anything you wanted to make a living, what would it be, and would you do it?

☐ Have you made any movement toward doing or being what you want to be?

☐ Can you identify what you are passionate about?

Now, expand upon your answers. [Engage fully in this inquiry. Discover something you did not see before and explore how you could experience satisfaction in each of these areas. **What would you need and what can you see has been missing until now** that keeps you from experiencing the ability to answer "yes" in all these areas?]

Chapter 10 (Cont'd)

Write your answers below or in your notebook...

_____

_____

_____

_____

_____

_____

_____

_____

_____

_____

_____

_____

_____

_____

_____

_____

_____

_____

_____

_____

_____

_____

_____

Chapter 10 (Cont'd)

STEP TWO:

Answer the following questions (Write your answers in your notebook):

1. What are two personal qualities or things about yourself that you take pride in…

_____

_____

_____

_____

_____

2. What do others say is outstanding about you?

_____

_____

_____

_____

_____

_____

3. What are a few of the things you do that are a contribution to others – and how do you do them?

_____

_____

_____

_____

Chapter 10 (Cont'd)

4. What ways do you enjoy expressing your appreciation for others?

_____
_____
_____
_____
_____
_____
_____
_____
_____
_____
_____
_____
_____
_____
_____
_____
_____
_____
_____

[**For example:** I like to cook for my family or I do errands for my friends or I write thank you notes for my brother or take my sister to school because she can't drive yet.]

Chapter 10 (Cont'd)

5. What activities have you enjoyed most in your life and that have given you the most satisfaction, pleasure and fulfillment? If you could do anything you wanted, what would it be?

_____

_____

_____

_____

_____

_____

_____

_____

_____

_____

_____

_____

_____

_____

STEP THREE:

From the List of Values or from any other source you prefer, select at least ten values that you believe are important or essential to you. [Think of them as the things that make life worth living and if you could not have them in your life, you would find it unsatisfying and unfulfilling. Keep that list in front of you as you do the next exercise "Creating Your Personal Mission Statement".]

Chapter 10 (Cont'd)

LIST OF VALUES

Hard work	Honesty	Selflessness
Volunteering	Donating money	Donating energy
Industriousness	Integrity	Donating Time
Creativity	Love	Hard Work
Endurance	Intelligence	Ethics
Problem-Solving	Compassion	Philanthropy
Friendship	Spirituality	Lifelong Learning
Family	Devoutness	Health & Wellness
Positive Attitude	Daring	Art
Calmness	Religion	Generosity
Innovation	Altruism	Self-Control
Empathy	Belief in God	Mindfulness
Being analytical	Integrity	Adventure
Optimism	Showing Affection	Imagination
Change	Attractiveness	Freedom
Contemplation	Charity	Innovation
Teaching Others	Education	Harmony
Belonging	Maturity	Beauty
Religion	Selflessness	Forward Thinking
Sympathy	Optimism	Exploration
Reasonableness	Harmony	Homeschooling
Philosophy	Realism	Acceptance
Activism	Idealism	Accomplishment
Adaptability	Humor	Accountability
Flexibility	Assertiveness	Success
Agility	Playfulness	Boldness
Affluence	Candor	Fame

Chapter 10 (Cont'd)

My Core Values...

1.

2.

3.

4.

5.

6.

7.

8.

9.

10.

Chapter 10 (Cont'd)

EXERCISE: Creating Your Personal Mission Statement

PICTURE THE FOLLOWING:

You are on a ship, traveling to a vacation destination and you are having a great time.

The Captain has called all of you into the main cabin and has said he has an announcement.

Here is what he says:

"Ladies and Gentlemen: I am sorry to announce that we have an onboard emergency and will have to abandon ship. However, it has become clear that we have limited space about the lifeboats. There is only enough room for each person to take with them 6 values. The rest will have to be abandoned and left behind.

At this time, you are to take a pen and strike through the five values that are least important to you and that you are willing to leave behind. I will be back with further instructions in 3 minutes."

Your Captain arrives back in 3 minutes:

"Ladies and Gentlemen: I am sorry to announce that we have had further bad news.

Chapter 10 (Cont'd)

One of the lifeboats that we thought we could use is no longer available – it has been sunk.

It is now evident that you may not bring with you 6 values as originally thought, you may only bring your top four. Please eliminate all others at this time. I will be back with further instructions in 2 minutes as we will begin to cast off."

Your Captain arrives back in 2 minutes:

"Ladies and Gentlemen; I have good news – we are about to get underway and while we have one more bit of bad news, it seems as if we will all survive. The only requirement is that you eliminate four more values and **select only the top two**. If you can do so immediately, we will begin to load the lifeboats. If you fail to do so, we will be forced to leave you behind. Please do this now – you have one minute to complete this task."

Are you finished?
Ok, Great – Let's go!

Ok, Scenario over.
Now, looking at the values you retained, what did you discover about yourself and what is important to you?

Chapter 10 (Cont'd)

Write your answers here or in your notebook.

_____

_____

_____

_____

_____

_____

_____

_____

_____

_____

_____

_____

_____

_____

_____

_____

_____

_____

_____

_____

_____

_____

_____

_____

Chapter 10 (Cont'd)

It is clear that these two remaining values are important as you create your new future. Utilizing these two values and what you discovered about yourself in answering the previous questions, how can you incorporate them into an inspiring personal purpose/mission statement? This statement will lead you on a path forward as you create your new, transformed life. It should touch, move and inspire you. It should give you direction and a place to stand in making choices and decisions as you create your new future.

STEP FOUR:

The next step is to identify areas about which you are passionate or in which you want to make a contribution. **For example:**

1. The world in general
2. In the lives of friends and family
3. In your community
4. With your fellow workers, employees or employers

STEP FIVE:

Make a list of nouns, adjectives, adverbs and verbs - words that inspire and move you: Here are a few examples:

Nouns:

Man, woman, people, countries, lives, hearts, minds, commitments, integrity, family, country, community, lifetime, possibilities, achievements, honor, love, truth, loyalty, satisfaction, fulfillment

Chapter 10 (Cont'd)

Adjectives:

Happy, generous, beneficial, possible, young, old, wealthy, poor, successful, needy, impassioned

Verbs:

Going, coming, make, create, design, inspire, enrich, give, take, donate, commit to, deserve, lift up, raise, admire, contribute, love, feed, walk, run, reach

Adverbs:

Happily, satisfactorily, successfully, quickly, effectively, passionately, essentially, unequivocally,

Begin to make a list of those words that most move you and put them together in a sentence or two that speaks to your passion and your commitment.

Keep in mind that it is YOUR personal mission statement; and your unique position in the world that you want to express.

A personal purpose or mission statement provides clarity and gives you a sense of purpose. It defines who you are and how you will live.

Here are a few powerful statements that have inspired others…

Chapter 10 (Cont'd)

Historian: "To educate, motivate and enable myself and all those who know me to achieve self-actualization and become everything I was destined to be."

Teacher: "My mission in life is to serve God by being a Beacon of Light, A Bridge of Understanding, a Tower of Integrity, and a Castle of Realized Dreams."

Writer, Coach: "I am committed that every conversation I have with anyone leaves them with a new possibility and opening for action they didn't see before we spoke."

Psychotherapist: "I will live everyday with Integrity and vow to consistently make a positive difference in the lives of others utilizing my knowledge for the good of all people."

Attorney: "My mission is to learn and understand my clients' needs and the external factors affecting them so that I can aggressively and professionally represent them throughout the legal process."

Keep in mind that when you are satisfied in life, your future is based on those values that mean the most to you - Without these, you would fail to thrive and would remain dissatisfied with your life.

Chapter 10 (Cont'd)

An Important Thought

Remember that a mission statement is always a work in progress and it can change over time, depending on what is happening or what you are creating in your life. Some change substantially over time and some never change in essence, merely in minor ways. Setting aside some time every year to review your choices, your goals and objectives and your purpose/mission statement will allow you to remain "in the present" and always engaged in the moment rather than "stuck" in something you decided in the past.

Now that you have created your personal purpose/mission statement, here is the 2nd exercise.

Designing your new future: Standing in the purpose you have created for your life, you can now design a new future - with no past to limit your possibilities!

Have fun doing it and let your imagination take off!

Chapter 10 (Cont'd)

Do the following:

Visualize how you want your life to be five years from now. You may not be clear exactly what you will be doing; however, you can be clear what you will have in your life and what you will be experiencing from the perspective of quality, happiness and all the things that would be present for you. Do this by answering the following questions:

Five years from now, if life were exactly the way you want it to be...

A. Where would you be living (describe what the physical place would be like)? A lake, the ocean, a mountain? Just picture it in your mind and jot down your answers below.

_____

_____

_____

_____

_____

_____

_____

_____

_____

_____

Chapter 10 (Cont'd)

B. What would your surroundings look like, what would you be
   wearing, eating, experiencing?

_____

_____

_____

_____

_____

_____

C. What are some of the activities and things you would   be doing
   and what would you be engaged in right now?

_____

_____

_____

_____

D. What would your lifestyle be like? Your work environment?

_____

_____

_____

_____

_____

Chapter 10 (Cont'd)

_____

_____

_____

_____

_____

_____

_____

E. What kind of experiences would you be having?

_____

_____

_____

_____

_____

_____

_____

F. What kind of car would you be driving? What would you be
   eating?

_____

_____

_____

_____

_____

_____

Chapter 10 (Cont'd)

Spend some time really creating everything you can about your ultimate life five years from now.

Now that you are clearer about what you want your life to look like, **explore what kind of work you might be doing.** Have it be as specific as you can – it doesn't have to be "realistic." Remember, when you get realistic, <u>you are looking toward the past to determine your future.</u> It should be doing something that fulfills your purpose or mission in life or at the very least is related in some way to accomplishing that. Close your eyes and envision what that looks and feels like.

Next, now that you have a **complete picture of your life** five years from today, standing THERE, **look backwards**; put yourself **back one year** in time.

Imagine: It is five years from now and you have everything you want.

What would you have been doing one year ago to make this five-year goal happen?

_____

_____

_____

_____

Chapter 10 (Cont'd)

•   Where would you have been living then?

_____

_____

_____

_____

_____

•   What would you be engaged in that, one year from today, you would have to have been doing so that could have been accomplished?

_____

_____

_____

_____

_____

_____

_____

Imagine: It is now <u>four years</u> from now and you are on the road to have everything you want in one more year. **(Repeat steps A through F again)**

Now, step back one more year, year three. **[Repeat steps A through F again]**

Chapter 10 (Cont'd)

> Now, step back one more year, year two. **(Repeat steps A through F again)**
>
> Now step back one more year, year one. **(Repeat steps A through F again)**
>
> Now look at your **present... look at life today.** Given what you said you wanted to happen five years from today**, are you engaged in those things that could give you that result?**
>
> If not, that is fine; you *now* know that you can take the steps you need to get you there!

Congratulations! – THAT is what it is like to stand in the present - with no past - creating your future!

This is the most powerful way to establish those things going forward that will bring you what you want; rather than looking to the past. This exercise can be used for many different things; especially in completing projects. **Just commit to it**; stand in your project's completion (the future) and walk yourself back: You will see everything you need to do to successfully complete anything! *Good work!*

You are now ready for your Chapter 10 Assignment!

CHAPTER 10 – AFFIRMACTIONS & ASSIGNMENT

Wow – You are almost there – You are beginning the completion of Chapter 10 …

What is that like? How do you feel in this moment? What have you learned? (Take a minute or two here to write one or two sentences about your thoughts at this moment… (Not too much though, you still have one more chapter to go, Dear Reader!)

_____

_____

_____

_____

_____

_____

So now, let's take a look at your Affirmation for Chapter 10

AFFIRM: What are you committed to creating in the way of "Being Here Now" this week? It could be anything from "Who I am is someone present to the joy and fulfillment of being alive in this moment and no other." Or "I am present in every moment to what is actually happening or occurring in this "now" moment and only in this moment "right now!"

Chapter 10 (Cont'd)

_____

_____

_____

_____

_____

To practice empowering yourself in creating being here, right now, in the present moment, every day this week, what would you say each time, and how would you say it?

ACTION: Now, what action(s) will you take each day to make this Affirmation real for you?

_____

_____

_____

_____

_____

_____

_____

_____

_____

_____

_____

Chapter 10 (Cont'd)

It's a philosophy of life. Practice. If you do this, something will change, what will change is that you will change, your life will change, and if you can change you, you can perhaps change the world.

Vivienne Westwood

EMPOWERMENT SUMMARY

The Art of Practicing

First, a few questions...

Have you done the activities at the end of every Chapter as you were instructed in the Introduction?

What have you learned that most stands out to you?

Where are you confused and what have you forgotten since beginning the book (Perhaps it will help to go back and review that Empowerment Chapter)?

What would you like to share with someone else – and who would that be?

Now, here are some intentions and clarity you may have discovered as a result of this material...

- The next step for you in what you want to create with what is left of your life...

- Some of the things that may have been missing in your relationships with others

Empowerment Summary (Cont'd)

- Some ways in which you have been limited by your thoughts and beliefs about the past and areas in which you can now be freer to discover possibilities

- People you would like to tell how much you value and love them and the difference they have made in your life

- People who no longer will get in your way or bother you because you have let go of your anger or hostility toward them

- People you have forgiven because you know that the anger you created was from a story you made up and not from something they said or did

- A new path to a future endeavor

- Some freedom in an area of life where you have been constrained in the past

By the way, wherever you are in your journey is exactly the right place.

Are you surprised?

Did you expect to read that, or did you expect repercussions as a result of not having fulfilled your assignments as designed?

Empowerment Summary (Cont'd)

Remember, in the Introduction, I said if you do not do the assignments as designed and in order, you forfeit the right to expect the results - and you may not achieve the "transformation" in being I promised?

Well, at this point in your journey, you could be in one of several places...Let me enumerate a few of those here...

(1) You could be one of the lucky ones –someone who did not complete the exercises in order, who did not perform your AffirmActions as instructed - yet still you did find enlightenment!

If that is the case - you are definitely one of the lucky ones and are to be congratulated, you lucky devil!

(2) On the other hand, if you DID complete the program and did perform the exercises as prescribed and *still* find yourself - at this juncture - feeling let down, disappointed or, worse still, dissatisfied by the time you have gotten to this point in the program, you have only to contact me, as the author of this program and, if you are willing,

Empowerment Summary (Cont'd)

I will give you a one-hour, complimentary coaching session and work with you to achieve clarity, answer your questions AND get to the source of where you may be stuck.

(3) Finally, If, indeed, you followed the directions, did all the exercises and have discovered a new, transformed way of being, I invite you to also go to the end of Chapter 10 and contact me; let me know what you discovered and experienced as a result of having taken this program.

Only then will I know that my time and words have made the kind of difference I intended as I sit here writing this today. I will also request that you give me a testimonial so that others can experience the freedom that – hopefully – you are feeling today.

I suppose there may be other conditions in which you, Dear Reader, now find yourself – and you would like to let me know about that. I am certainly open to hearing it all.

I invite you, however, before any of you contact me, to take a good look at what you have or have not accomplished and **review Empowerment Chapter 1**. You remember, when we looked at the value of taking responsibility for everything in your world. Keep in mind to remove blame or fault and look only at being the source for everything you have or don't have.

Empowerment Summary (Cont'd)

Then, look to see what YOU can do to secure the transformation you - and everyone living on this planet - deserve.

Once you have reviewed Empowerment Chapter 1, complete your assignment for your Empowerment Summary Chapter.

There are still two more subjects to tackle, I believe, before we close...

One is a subject that I have been warned to avoid – since it can be "controversial." However, you may have noticed by now that I am not exactly one to shy away from odd and controversial subjects, so I think I will take on just this one more.

It's about another "G" word (Remember? the first was Gratitude).

That's right – On the subject of "God," and the Divine, I thought it might be a worthwhile addition to a book on transformation and "ontology" – the being of human beings; especially since we human beings seem to spend a lot of time thinking and talking about this particular subject.

As it turns out, recently a friend of mine, in a conversation about good and evil, asked me whether or not I believed in God.

Empowerment Summary (Cont'd)

While I have entertained that question at different times in my life and for many different reasons, this time it struck me as relevant and I decided that adding it here might be useful.

While I have often engaged in a dialogue about religion with friends and colleagues; it has always seemed to me that much harm has been done in the world in the name of it. I would never assume, however, that everyone should feel that way, nor would I presume that, for many, it is not a valuable or important aspect of their lives.

The same is true about belief in God or a "higher" power.

Now, getting into a religious conversation here is probably not very useful since I have no idea what practices you might find rewarding or valuable, as this has been – pretty much – a one-way conversation.

That said, I would also not unequivocally state that I don't believe that God - or whatever higher power there is – does or does not exist. I choose to think, at least at this moment in my life, that a higher power, if it does indeed exist, lives in each of us and that life began on this planet for a reason; I am just not egocentric enough to think that I can understand "the plan" or the reason, if, indeed, there is one.

Well, first let me say that I don't believe there is a white bearded, all knowing "God" hanging around, listening to our every word or answering our every prayer.

Empowerment Summary (Cont'd)

I believe it is more likely that each of us was endowed by some greater power with everything we need to create paradise - or hell - right here on earth (and sometimes, so far, at least it appears to me, we are not doing a very good job of heading in the right direction).

I believe Earth and human life was a gift; and that whatever made it possible for life to occur, here on this planet, was not of this planet. I am struck every day by the beauty and perfection of how "life" works and the amazing gifts that some human beings show in the depth of goodness and strength of character they display.

It just seems, to me, that we do not all use our capabilities to the degree that's possible - *that is what makes us "human."* I believe that we make our own heaven and hell, right here on earth, and we were given the tools to do so - and the choices are ours. I also like what Wayne Dyer said about spirituality and religion…

"Your destiny is to become a co-creator with God and to treasure the sanctity of all that comes into this world of form that we call home, but which is only a transitory stopping place"

Wayne Dyer (In Manifesting Your Spiritual Destiny)

Empowerment Summary (Cont'd)

AND, in speaking about transitory states, I have something else to add to all of this transformational mumbo jumbo... Are you ready?

The word **transitory** has a very special meaning in the world of NOW... You know, the one we have been exploring for a while.

What I want to say about that is one word...

ENTROPY.

How does Entropy affect our lives, what exactly is it and why am I bringing it up here?

Well, it's is a natural law – just like the Law of Gravity. Let go of something you are holding in your hand and it will drop to the next lower surface. And, like gravity, entropy is another such natural Law of the Universe; it exists whether you believe in it or not.

Have you ever noticed that when you move, and the movers come in to move the refrigerator, when they pull it away from the wall, the floor underneath is usually pretty grimy even though you have never dropped anything under or walked on it? Or under the washer/dryer? Or even, sometimes under the bed?

Empowerment Summary (Cont'd)

Another thing to look at when we talk about this subject is when you put something away in an attic and then you go to look at it years later, it just doesn't usually look the same. The colors have faded, or the fabric looks yellowed, or the photos look less clear?

This kind of deterioration is the result of "entropy" and here is the working definition:

> **Entropy: Entropy could be said to be the tendency for all matter and energy in the universe to devolve toward a state of inert uniformity.** It is the Inevitable and steady deterioration of a system or society.

How that shows up in reality is that, when left alone, things deteriorate. That includes people. So, like the old "use it or lose it" philosophy, entropy will cause anything not in use to degenerate. This includes knowledge and the changes you are putting in place in your lives out of the work you are doing in this program.

If you fail to continue practicing what you are learning and habituate the new changes into your life, what will tend to happen is that your new-found wisdom will become less and less evident to you, the transformation you experience will become less and less real and you are likely to slip back into being "comfortable" with the old way of "being" that you have experienced in your past.

Empowerment Summary (Cont'd)

So, Dear Reader, stay in the flow, continue to practice your AffirmActions, being in the here and now, creating the future from the present and creating your new "reality" and you will continue to grow and prosper. Stop - and entropy will step in and take over!

Stay in action and continue to create your transformed life!

Now, finally, just a few questions for you to dwell in before I let you go...

- Are you clearer about what is possible for you?
- Have you posted your Personal Mission Statement somewhere visible, so that you can read it every day?
- Are you continuing with your AffirmActions on a daily basis?

After all, now that we have completed this very challenging work together (I say together because I feel that I will have been with you the entire time), I think it is appropriate for me to give you some final words....

Unfortunately, there is some bad news...

Empowerment Summary (Cont'd)

Here it is, the Bad News...

(Yes, that's right. I am the bearer of bad news.)

I did not give this to you in the beginning because I feared you would not complete the book. But now that you have done so, I feel I must be honest with you.

Please sit down - if you are not already seated.

I believe I shared with you in the beginning when you first picked up this book, that I have been doing this transformational work for more than 30 years. And, every year that I do it, I get more grounded in the wonderful possibility that transformation has offered me each and every day. Having said that, each and every day, I wake up and, for a moment... just a moment... I wait.

I wait... hoping that the man of my dreams will walk through the door. I wait... hoping for my life to be the glorious success I had hoped for when I was growing up.

I wait for all my wishes to have come true while I slept. I wait breathless - as I open my bank account online, hoping that a miracle has occurred and that my savings is full to overflowing with all the money I could possibly ever want or need.

Empowerment Summary (Cont'd)

And then I smile – **because none of that has happened.**

I smile because I am transformed - and I realize I am hoping – and not living in THIS moment. This moment... the only moment I really have. The only moment I am alive – and well – and loved – and living a life I create...moment by moment.

And then I laugh – I laugh at the automatic, mechanistic workings of my mind. A mind that keeps me safe, that at the same time is my greatest gift and my greatest challenge. I embrace my foolishness, my mind hoping for the impossible – and I embrace my heart – loving my life and all the challenges every day brings – and I am grateful for another day to practice.

Because, Dear Reader – and friend – truly, all there is to do is practice.

Practice living in THIS moment, in this reality, in the present – and taking full responsibility for the life I have been given - one moment at a time. Loving it, resisting it, sometimes wishing it were different, and always, always grateful for every single moment of it.

So, while our work together is drawing to an end, your work on living a transformed life will never be done. You will remain, forever, as you are now... the same human being - and that is the bad AND the good news

Empowerment Summary (Cont'd)

After more than 30 years of doing this work of being human, it comes down to this... **Practice every day what you have learned here**. The enlightenment will come – and it will go.

You will have moments when you forget everything you have read and I have said. And then you will remember. You will notice somewhere you are not taking 100% responsibility – You have been blaming someone – or yourself. You have forgotten who you are and how powerful you can be.

And then you will remember – and you will clean it up by owning your part.

Keep this book handy…and begin again. It will all come back to you – it is easier the second time around, and the third, and every time thereafter.

That, Dear Reader, is the joy - and dilemma - of being human.

I send you, along with this book, my deep love and regard. You may wonder how I can say that, never having met you. But I know who you are. If you have picked up this book, there was a longing in you – as there was in me – for more. To be more – and to give more. And for that I love you.

Empowerment Summary (Cont'd)

I may not see you as you read these pages, but I carry you and all human beings who long for a world that works for everyone; I carry you in my heart. Werner said that many years ago – and it lives with me still.

Keep practicing – Entropy is not far behind!

As you have learned throughout this book, being "human" carries with it many "built in" gifts and pitfalls.

By writing this book, I remain committed to promoting what I see are the amazing possibilities of "human being" and of the massive good of which we are capable.

I hope that I have contributed something valuable for you in these past pages: That you will have learned something useful from our work together and that your choices - and mine - will improve our relationships, create transformation on the planet, and that, together, we can design the kind of world we want for ourselves and those whom we love.

I invite you to share what you have learned; by that I mean share your hearts with those people in your life you love and cherish. Let them know how much they mean to you and what you have gotten from these pages about trust, about responsibility, about integrity and about living a life you love.

Empowerment Summary (Cont'd)

Share with them that you discovered there is more to you than your "mind" and that you – (and they) – have a choice – always – whether to do the right thing, the ethical thing, and to "BE" everything they want to be, without having to give up anything - other than "being right" – to make a difference on the planet.

To further your efforts on that behalf, I have your final assignment. Here is a list of things you can do (Do I hear a "Yay" from the audience?). **Pick at least one each and every day – and live the transformation you have created for yourself in reading and working through these pages.**

Begin ...

Empowerment Summary (Cont'd)

- Eliminate procrastination now!

- Be decisive – Create goals for yourself that empower you and leave you fulfilled.

- Always be willing to change, to grow, to remain open to seeing your "blind-spots."

- Remain true to yourself and your dreams and allow others to do the same.

- Take risks!

- Be a life-long learner – Take what you learned from this book and **share it with others**.

- **Live life from Level 3 Responsibility** – even if your limbic brain tells you the opposite.

- Be trustworthy & dependable – so that you can trust others; remember, it begins with you.

- Respect the humanity of everyone.

- Never give up – on yourself or on others.

- Speak to the other person's listening rather than to your "need" to be heard.

- **Appreciate THIS moment – it is the ONLY one you have!**

- Own it ALL – **Be powerful!**

- Keep climbing the mountain (*Integrity, remember?*)

Empowerment Summary (Cont'd)

- **Be willing to say…**
  - I'm sorry
  - I'm wrong
  - I appreciate you
  - I'm proud of you
  - What do YOU see about this?
  - How can I help?
  - Thank you
  - **…and I love you**

I'd like to close with a quote from one of my favorite radio shows, *News from Lake Woebegone*, as they closed each remarkable show for years…

"Be well, do good work, and keep in touch."

If you wish to contact me for any reason or to inquire about coaching, please drop me an email at Info@TheBookofBeing.com and I will be happy to respond.

Empowerment Summary (Cont'd)

As human beings, our greatness lies not so much in being able to remake the world - this is the myth of the atomic age - as in being able to remake ourselves.

Mahatma Gandhi

EPILOGUE

Thank you , Geoff Owen, for beginning this journey with me – May success follow you always, and thank you, Werner, for all the blessings you have brought into my life.

I began this book with a mention of Werner Erhard and I end it with him as well. As the man who first introduced me to transformation, he is someone to whom millions of people will be forever grateful.

In sharing what he saw about the difference in living as an ordinary human being without the possibility of transformation and one who has experienced it, he said…

*"**We can discover another possibility: living in a way, now, moment to moment, that makes a difference to life.** We discover that as human beings we can live in a possibility instead of in what we have inherited, that instead of just being a human being because we were born that way, we can declare the possibility of being for human beings. **This is the work of transformation: bringing forth a breakthrough in the possibility of being human.**"*

Werner Erhard

Epilogue (Cont'd)

I believe this quote of Werner's sums up my purpose for writing this book for you, Dear Reader; it was my dream of giving you this gift of possibility. **Thank you for trusting me to deliver that dream.**

P.S. I awoke one morning shortly after finishing this book with an epiphany; one that I wanted to share with you. So, after much deliberation – and consternation from my publisher – I have decided to add something here. Consider it my gift… A Talisman of sorts. I give it to you in hopes that, in the future, as you remember this book (which I hope you will), you will remember as well this little "gem of wisdom**."**

It is a "Visual" which I will leave with you, in hopes that it will inspire you to continue your journey into "Being" all that you wish to be. I call it the "Hierarchy of Being."

I hope you enjoy it!

If you wish to let me know what you thought of my parting gift, anything about my book, or inquire into coaching sessions, you can contact me at www.theBookofBeing.com or you can email me at Lee@TheBookofBeing.com. And, if you have an interest in continuing your work in transformation, check out www.Landmarkworldwide.com for the work that Werner Erhard began many years ago (and tell them I sent you!).

Epilogue (Cont'd)

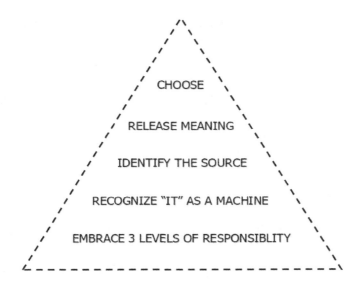

Hierarchy of Being

While "being" is not a linear process, I believe this hierarchy exists and – like Maslow's theory – can be helpful to define where each of us is in our journey to finding "Self" and the gift of "Being" in the moment. Here is a brief explanation of this visual.

As you will experience, "being" is not linear in nature; however, there IS a journey or path to follow... **Each level – once fulfilled – leads to the next.** We can be anywhere - at any time - on the continuum, from bottom to top; and each choice we make brings us closer to "being" our true Selves and to knowing we are the choices we make. Being conscious and being "in the moment" begins with owning it all – beginning with the three levels of Responsibility.

See additional Supplementary Materials and "A Gift" on the following pages.

SUPPLEMENTARY MATERIALS

[The remaining pages of the book will have answers to questions, extra handouts, references to online resources, etc., as well as the keys to Hidden Pictures and the Positive Reframing Exercises from the book.]

From Page 73: a reference to Scientific Information about the Brain – www. http://thebrain.mcgill.ca

THE EVOLUTIONARY LAYERS OF THE HUMAN BRAIN

The first time you observe the anatomy of the human brain, its many folds and overlapping structures can seem very confusing, and you may wonder what they all mean. But just like the anatomy of any other organ or organism, the anatomy of the brain becomes much clearer and more meaningful when you examine it in light of the evolutionary processes that created it.

Probably the best-known model for understanding the structure of the brain in relation to its evolutionary history is the famous triune brain theory, which was developed by Paul MacLean and became very influential in the 1960s. Over the years since, however, several elements of this model have had to be revised in light of more recent neuroanatomical studies (see the first two history modules, to the left). Keeping this in mind, MacLean's original model distinguished three different brains that appeared successively during evolution:

These three parts of the brain do not operate independently of one another. They have established numerous interconnections through which they influence one another.

The reptilian brain, the oldest of the three, controls the body's vital functions such as heart rate, breathing, body temperature and balance. Our reptilian brain includes the main structures found in a reptile's brain: the brainstem and the cerebellum. The reptilian brain is reliable but tends to be somewhat rigid and compulsive.	The limbic brain emerged in the first mammals. It can record memories of behaviours that produced agreeable and disagreeable experiences, so it is responsible for what are called emotions in human beings. The main structures of the limbic brain are the hippocampus, the amygdala, and the hypothalamus. The limbic brain is the seat of the value judgments that we make, often unconsciously, that exert such a strong influence on our behaviour.	The neocortex first assumed importance in primates and culminated in the human brain with its two large cerebral hemispheres that play such a dominant role. These hemispheres have been responsible for the development of human language, abstract thought, imagination, and consciousness. The neocortex is flexible and has almost infinite learning abilities. The neocortex is also what has enabled human cultures to develop.

Supplementary Materials (Cont'd)

Key to Hidden Pictures

In this big picture find the toothbrush, top hat, butterfly, sailboat, teacup...

Supplementary Materials (Cont'd)

POSITIVE REFRAMING EXERCISE [KEY]

1. I think we need more milk for the week.

2. I will be there after 7 AM.

3. I want you to understand the point I am making.

4. I need you to speak a little louder.

5. I can only wait 20 minutes for you.

6. I prefer another color dress on you - or - I like you better in a different dress.

7. Remember to be on time tonight – it's important!

8. Explain it clearly [or Create clarity].

9. Remember to bring the book.

10. We should agree with our customers.

> **NOTE:** #11 is tricky. You will note that because people are usually so negative, they will come up with a negative approach to this statement. That she should be fired or she is bad or something like that - when in reality, she is merely doing something OTHER than her job - it could even be in addition to or instead of - but people usually fail to think of that. This is just an interesting sidelight so that you can see how prone to negativity we are!

11. *She is doing something other than her job.*

12. It's easy to do it correctly.

13. We should cooperate with each other.

Supplementary Materials (Cont'd)

Resource Document on INTEGRITY

Integrity as a way of being and as a distinction means "being whole and complete, with nothing and no one left out. It means doing what you said you would do when you said you would do it; honoring your word and being responsible for cleaning it up when you do not."

Reminder: Using the metaphor we used earlier to describe the experience of integrity…

When a bicycle wheel is missing a spoke or the rim is bent; the wheel will most likely continue to turn and the bike will continue move. However, it will not roll in a straight direction. It will tend to steer right or left and go off track. You may eventually move ahead but you will not get to the destination you want without a great deal more work – or possibly not at all, since you may have a breakdown along the way when the bike refuses to move at all because the wheel begins rubbing against the fender. At the least, movement will be slow as there will be friction where the moving parts rub against each other.

Life without integrity is similar. You may keep moving forward, but your speed will be diminished, and you will not move in a direct route to your destination. It is likely that you will frequently veer off course and have to put in a great deal more effort and energy in order to get back on course, and to, eventually, reach your destination – if ever.

Supplementary Materials (Cont'd)

When you live with an awareness of integrity and a willingness to be looking for where it needs to be raised, your journey will be smoother, with less detours. Continually looking at where your integrity can be increased can make a difference in your life's journey, and in the process, will keep you rolling more smoothly toward your goals.

See the **Personal Integrity Worksheet** on the next page. I invite you to create something similar and make a habit of using it every day! You WILL notice a difference in what you accomplish and your experience of life.

Supplementary Materials (Cont'd)

Book of Being
Integrity Worksheet

TODAY'S DATE: _____

	Basic Integrity (Personal)	Yes	No	By When?	What is there to Communicate or Actions to take?
1	My physical presentation meets my standards				
2	My finances are in order (Balanced checkbook, all $ accounted for)				
3	My eating is consistent w/my commitments				
4	My exercising is consistent w/my commitments				
5	I am an 8 or above with my friends, family, and associates				
6	I have a clear work space for producing breakthrough results				
7	Next week is set up for maximum productivity				
8	I am living consistent with the commitments I set for this year				
9	My life is a demonstration of breaking through limitations & beliefs				
10	Are there integrity issues impacting me?				
11	Actions I will take to restore my integrity:				
12					
13					
14	My commitments for LAST WEEK & did I fulfill on them?				
15	What do I need to do to declare myself complete for last week?				

Supplementary Materials (Cont'd)

ON GRATITUDE

Albert Schweitzer

"At times, our own light goes out and is rekindled by a spark from another person. Each of us has cause to think with deep gratitude of those who have lighted the flame within us."

Buddha
"Let us rise up and be thankful, for if we didn't learn a lot today, at least we learned a little, and if we didn't learn a little, at least we didn't get sick, and if we got sick, at least we didn't die; so, let us all be thankful."

Margaret Cousins
"Appreciation can make a day, even change a life. Your willingness to put it into words is all that is necessary."

John F. Kennedy

"As we express our gratitude, we must never forget that the highest appreciation is not to utter words, but to live by them."

Cicero

"Gratitude is not only the greatest of virtues, but the parent of all the others."

See "**An Exercise in Gratitude**" on the next page...

THE BOOK OF BEING...

A Gift for You!

An Exercise in Gratitude... Ask yourself the following questions:

- How does <u>expressing</u> gratitude affect your ability to <u>experience</u> gratitude?
    - Expressing gratitude and appreciation brings us present to gratitude – beyond the gratitude for any specific example.

- Where is gratitude present in your life?
    - What are the areas for which you are clearly grateful?

- Where in your life is it challenging to create gratitude?
    - What do you see about those areas?
    - Does your reluctance or resistance to being grateful for those areas have any benefit to you?

        - Can you reveal a belief that if you see value in something you don't particularly want it will cause you to be stuck with its remaining that way?

        - Is it possible that finding value in something you don't want will alter your experience of having it?

A Gift for You! (Cont'd)

- What is the benefit of experiencing gratitude in all areas of your life?

- Keep in mind that "what you resist, persists."

- Dissatisfaction attracts more dissatisfaction!

- Gratitude attracts more gratitude -- and more for which to be grateful.

- What does the context of gratitude make available?
  - It's its own reward; it feels great to be grateful.
  - It's not possible to be grateful and unhappy at the same time!
  - Gratitude is closely tied to love and is an expression of the Divine.
  - Gratitude is the ideal condition for attracting Miracles!

Explore what opens up for you when you create gratitude for everything in your life and are thankful every morning for the things that you have.

What can you see is possible if gratitude in your life were a constant?

A Gift for You! (Cont'd)

What would it take for you to live in and from gratitude at all times? (In other words, what are the access points to keep returning to a state of gratitude?)

In the excerpt from the book, <u>Pronoia Is the Antidote to Paranoia; How the Whole World is Conspiring to Shower You with Blessings</u> by Rob Breszny, you can read about the amazing, infinite blessings that we all have before we even get to the specifics of our own lives!

What are some ways that you can bring yourself present to gratitude for your life and to appreciate those things we tend to take for granted?

Some possibilities:
- Being in nature, a favorite place to get touch with gratitude
- Being with or communicating with a favorite person
- Being in the presence of great art/music/literature, etc.
- Being in the presence of a baby or special pet
- Uplifting reading
- Creating a gratitude list
- Meditating
- Taking time for any favorite activity
- Acknowledging someone
- Being of service
- Dancing, singing
- Engaging in a favorite sport or creative activity

ABOUT THE AUTHOR

For 36 years, Lee has been studying transformation and the power of "being;" preparing to provide a pathway to freedom, satisfaction, fulfillment, and passion to anyone who is ready to embrace it.

Most importantly for her readers, she maintains that the path requires a *commitment* from the reader to change patterns and habits from the past, to engage and explore the source of those habits and their power to hold you back from *BEING* all that you can be. In "The Book of Being," she dares you to take it on – challenges you to explore your humanity – and reveal your future self; unrecognizable – and *unstoppable!*

Lee's broad range of abilities and expertise in communications, coaching, transformational studies, curriculum design, copywriting, and training make her an extraordinary author and consultant. Over the past 16 years, she has served as Director of Management Training to major corporations, designing executive leadership and management training programs, **corporate university curriculum, and business and personal growth programs,** which have contributed to the transformation of thousands of lives.

As a "ghost writer" for other authors and individuals in the entertainment and marketing industry, she has created and delivered numerous coaching programs for Law of Attraction luminaries and authors and has written training manuals, manuscripts, marketing & advertising copy, and articles on subjects as diverse as "Building Effective Teams," and "Creating Blended Families."

Her experience in coaching entrepreneurs and designing and delivering leadership effectiveness training spans multiple industries from high tech to beauty and from government agencies to educational faculties. These experiences have given her the expertise needed to understand how to speak and write effectively to a widely diverse audience.

She has raised three grown sons & currently lives in Austin, Texas where she writes, paints, sculpts and manages a lively coaching practice. Contact her at Lee@TheBookofBeing.com for more information or to schedule a coaching session.

Made in the USA
Coppell, TX
10 January 2022

71378726R10175